Emerging from the Mist:

Awakening the Balance of Female Empowerment in the World

by Jen Ward

ISBN-13: 978-1542359030

ISBN-10: 1542359031

01-12-2017: EDITION 1

02-10-2017: EDITION 2

THIS IS WHAT WE DO HERE TODAY

Every single person reading this book agreed to come together centuries ago when we all dispersed into the mist. We agreed to come back together when it was safe. We agreed to return to empowerment when the world so desperately needed to reawaken to the creativity, compassion, imagination and solace of its own stillness. We're fulfilling a promise we made to humanity to share our abilities in a mixture of synergy and passion to awaken those who still slumber and to heal the ills of apathy and indifference.

What happens here is a turning point in our level of awareness. Where all felt they were separate beings fighting merely to exist, many now lay down their swords and shields and feel the depth of their own worth. Where one once felt needy and depraved, they will now feel satiated by the love of their own abilities and eager to share. Where one was caught up in problems and stagnant complaints, they will be moved to solutions and the fluidity of empowering others. Mark this day. Mark this moment. Feel your presence enhance in your ability to move love through all the clogged pores of life.

This is what we do here.

INTRODUCTION

Healers Reunite

An echo fills the Ancient sky
There's heard one Universal cry
Percussions, movement, a rhythmic blend
Hands that heal, bodies mend
The dance to capture visions lost
Regain freedom at any cost
Broken lives we all endure
Remembering wholeness is the cure
To wash away the ills of man
Unite us with our tribe again
In this life few understand
What the Shaman woman can withstand
To ease the suffering of those she can
Heart to heart and hand to hand

These eons later old friends dispersed

To meet as strangers is their curse

Ways of remembering now dull and gray

All searching for the easy way

The healer steps forward in the artificial Light

To show the brilliance of true sight

Ancestors dance within with spirits of earth and wind

Enhance the process of remembering

All seekers of truth squint to see

The humble stance of the Shaman's decree

As she summons the spirits, blows away the pain

Calls love back to the earth again

With the bending of the Light

Others break through the night

Remembering their vows to reunite

As coaches and healers they re-gather their clan

Inspired to mend the broken land

We meet again across time and space

See recognition in a weary face

A fellow healer who endured at all cost

And many times thought that all was lost

Feel the blessings that do ensue

When one lost crusader learns there's two

Exponential healing has begun

Spiritual freedom is now rewon.

TABLE OF CONTENTS

How to Do the Taps

Here is how to do the tapping exercises that I share. I am energetically able to assist everyone who does the taps by moving out the stagnant energy that they release. Say each statement three times out loud while CONTINUOUSLY tapping on the top of your head at the crown chakra and say it a fourth time while tapping on your chest at the heart chakra. Say each word deliberately. They are not just words but a vibration that you are initiating to shift energy. Pause after each word. Say it in a commanding but even tone, not as a question. Forgo saying it in a singsong tone or with bravado. Say them all. Notice the semi-colon before "in all moments." This is to emphasize the pause before those three words.

1: BEING BEAUTIFUL

Body Gratitude

Can you change how you think about your body? Instead of judging it on aesthetics, can you just admire it for the incredible journey that you are on together? Can you thank it for its strength and resilience? Can you be in its corner the way that it has been in yours? No one has been more devoted to you than your own body. Can you just appreciate the fact that you have one and you get to be here in this physical world because of it?

Who cares if each hair is in place? Each hair is a receptor for the sensitivities that you have accrued. Who cares if the padding shifts positions? It cares about your comfort and safety, not about winning a prize of any kind. Who cares if you don't stand out because of what you look like? Maybe that was the divine plan all along. Everything that a dear friend has ever done for you, your own body has done and more. It has cried for you, laughed with you and left a trail of memories on its terrain as homage to the journey.

Perhaps the physical pain that you feel is the dejection that your body feels. Perhaps if you shift into gratitude for every muscle fiber, bone and corpuscle, your whole health will shift. Stop treating your own body like an indentured servant and start respecting it for the marvel that it is.

-Joy Love Abundance-

The bra is a burka for the breasts.

-Freedom Health Success-

Debunking Perfection

The holy men of history did a disservice to humanity as far as preaching about reaching the ultimate state of perfection. It confused the human species. Such perfection does not exist in the physical form. It made people feel unworthy and discouraged by not being able to reach perfection. It also held an invisible carrot in front of them, leading them away from their own empowerment towards an intangible goal of lofty heights.

This was not their plan. But it was the result. Male energy of its own accord is not going to reach its greatest potential without blending itself with female energy. The blending of the male and female energy in an expanded state of realization is what enlightenment is.

Reaching the blissful heights of higher dimensions by focusing all of your attention on leaving the body is done in male energy. It is a single-pointed driven goal. It takes a whole lot of discipline and a whole lot of drive to achieve it. Those who are not able to do this are left feeling inadequate and lost. Those who can achieve this can be spiritually smug if that is such a thing and sometimes unbalanced.

This goal to gain the highest perfection in the physical world has created such a warped social class. Those who are the richest, most beautiful and charismatic are the ones who are valued as if they have achieved some sort of perfection. They have not. The rich can become bullies to maintain their edge, the charismatic can become obnoxious in desperation to maintain their charm, and the beautiful will mutilate their faces and starve themselves in a desperate need to maintain beauty.

It is time to add the female energy back into the mix. It will enhance the quality of the experiences that we all have endured in mainstream society. It is a matter of setting different standards on what rich, charismatic and beautiful is. For me and many others, the polished, slick over-coached qualities that are valued in the media are nauseating. The overconfident person who has no compassion for the depth of what humanity endures is simply ugly to me.

The mainstream is starving for this depth of humanity to shine that only can be revealed when female energy is honored. Media tries to capture this whenever they pan in on a close-up of someone crying, or when they play tragic events over and over on the news, or when they depict aesthetically pleasing housewives or young women fighting. They have missed the mark.

The realness and organic goodness that is so alluring is someone who is kind when there is no audience. It is a quirky face or demeanor that is so fascinating to observe. It is a person so devoid of self-consciousness that they aren't even aware or concerned in how others view them. They are so caught up in their experience of each moment that no attention is focused elsewhere in a concern for how they are perceived.

This happens when a person is able to embrace all their gifts, talents and self-gratitude completely in the vessel that they are. They are loved, confident, abundant in so many peripheral ways and confident in their flawed vessel. The truth is perfection is a myth in the physical form. It is a fleeting state at best. But living, being, having and expressing perfection can happen in this imperfect form through immersing oneself in the moment and drawing everyone else into doing the same.

Real beauty and perfection is the exponential quality that draws the observer deeper and more completely into the moment. If you want to achieve spiritual perfection, it is not done by spending all your energy trying to leave the body. It is the total opposite. It is done by focusing all your attention, love and gratitude in the moment. It's expounding into exponential arenas while still being centered in your own skin.

-Joy Love Abundance-

How to See Beauty in Others

Beauty is subjective. Almost everyone sees beauty in flowers because they do nothing to offend the senses. They are safe to appreciate. They have never hurt anyone or caused pain other than the discomfort of allergies.

It is more difficult to see beauty in things that are threatening. A particular woman can seem beautiful to many, but if she has been deceitful or hurtful to someone, they may not see beauty anymore when they look at her.

People can actually train themselves to see beauty. It is a good practice. It is a prelude to experiencing love everywhere. When I was imprisoned, I had the most beautiful and loving experiences with nature. These are some of my most cherished memories.

Technique: Focus on something that you do not gauge as beautiful. See it from a different vantage point. Think about its journey and how it was created. Speculate about the life cycle of the item, person or aspect that you would not usually put attention on. See its place in the world and look at it from all angles. Do this until you can find beauty and value in it and can appreciate its existence. By practicing this technique, you will be more apt to find beauty and purpose in yourself.

Here are some taps to help:

(Say each statement three times while continuously tapping

on your head. Say it a fourth time while tapping on your chest. The semicolon before "in all moments" is there to remind you to pause.)

"I see beauty and value in all, including myself; in all moments."

"I make space in this world for infinite beauty; in all moments."

"I release deducing beauty to a competition; in all moments."

"I remove all blockages to seeing beauty in all; in all moments."

"I stretch my capacity to see and enhance beauty in all; in all moments."

If these taps were effective, do them again and switch out the word beauty for Love, Abundance, Joy and Freedom.

-Freedom Health Success-

Original Intention of Beauty Products

Many Beauty practices and shows about divas are another way to enslave female energy. Just like the fashion obsession and shoe obsession. You know why high-heel pumps are a form of enslavement? They prevent female energy from being grounded in the mother earth. It is a form of choosing outer beauty over female empowerment.

-Joy Love Abundance-

Beauty

Who we are in the physical realm is such a small component of who we really are. It is literally a tip of our iceberg. To focus so much of our attention on our physical form is a distraction from our true nature and our own truth. For us to be deceived into focusing so much attention on our body is an intentional form of distraction. It keeps us enslaved in denial of our true dynamic self. It is a lie. It is the perfect prison because we, ourselves, keep ourselves contained.

All the energy focused on our weight, features, wardrobe, hair texture, and all the accessories that that entails, is us buying into the lie. The lie is that we need to do anything outwardly to enhance our own beauty. Beauty is our innate nature.

Beauty is love, honor, kindness, integrity and truth. To be those things is to enhance that inner beauty that is unmatched by any synthetic process.

-Freedom Health Success-

The Beauty of Your Own Essence

There is no crime in making yourself invisible as a survival tool along the way. We have all had to use that as a coping mechanism. The crime and violation to humanity is you staying stuck in believing the lie. To believe you are worthless, powerless, unable to manifest simple joy, love and abundance is a travesty to soul's conviction.

We are more than the sum of our parts. We are exponentially uplifted into the resonance of pure bliss when we understand our own divine abilities and makeup. This happens exponentially and unequivocally with greater avail when each component, each individual carries the greatness of their own worth into the mix.

When you step away from the diminishing stance that you have held, you uplift humanity. When you gather up your greatness and uncover your gifts, you uplift humanity. When you choose simple kindness over the gluttony of ego and pride, you uplift humanity. When you live a life of simple joy, unbeknownst or uncaring of what others do, you shine a spotlight on yourself in the invisible realms.

Those who clamor with accomplishments and gaudy appeal offend the sweetness of the invisible realms. You, in your quiet venture and nobility of purpose, are wrapped in a shroud of light. Each decision of substance that takes others into consideration highlights your beautiful features.

Each choice that enhances the collective, is praised and applauded in the true arena of the higher order.

When did sincerity become so disdained? When did noble intentions become obsolete? When did simple goodness go out of style? You, in your awakened awareness, are timelessly and effortlessly unadulterated. The more you recognize it and the more you embrace it in yourself, the more you allow others to embrace the brilliancy of their own worth. You are not nothing. You are EVERYTHING in the context that matters.

If you can't quite embrace your empowerment for yourself, please do it for all the millions of those waiting to step out of the shadows of being deemed a nothing. Use your new conviction to coax them into the Love. In this way, you are a visionary and a humanitarian. You, in your efforts, have the ability to dry up the shadows of this world and bring all others into the Love. You hold all of humanity in your cupped hands when you embrace with all sincerity the beauty of your own essence.

-Joy Love Abundance-

What It Takes to Feel Pretty

Today, I facilitated a session with a beautiful, talented fourteen-year old girl who started acting out. She is loved and nurtured by two responsible parents. But she started to smoke and experiment with alcohol and pot. To so many, it would be dismissed as growing pains. But her mother was alarmed.

When I tuned into the child, I saw horrific images of a possible future. I alluded to them with the mother. The mother, who is very intuitive, said that she felt a similar fate may be in store. They were images of her being trafficked. It scared the mother enough to schedule an emergency session for her daughter.

The daughter, who had become defiant with her mother, complied to have a session with me. I facilitated it in person. Immediately, I asked her about the boy that was influencing her. She had played down the relationship with him to her mother, but they had a strong psychic connection from a past life. It was confusing her. She knew he wasn't a good person to be around, but she couldn't seem to help herself. It was very strong. Because of him, she was compelled to do things that her innocent life of fourteen years had no possible reason to support. She was very confused and was suffering at a deep level.

I saw her dynamism with this boy through other lifetimes. In a past lifetime, he was her pimp. She had been broken to his will in many lives. She had a string of horrific lifetimes that involved her giving her power over to him. I led her through some taps that resonated at a deep level to her. I was tough on her, but I was interrupting a deeply ingrained pattern.

"I release pissing away my childhood; in all moments."

"I release being bought and sold many times over; in all moments."

"I release the trauma of being a sex slave; in all moments."

"I release having Stockholm Syndrome; in all moments."

"I release being physically and energetically raped; in all moments."

I also went through the whole protocol of releasing her dynamics with the boy who was influencing her. I closed up her energy to him and retrieved all her attributes that he had taken from her. She was starting to feel like things could be better.

Without her telling me, I told her things that her mother didn't even know. I told her how I know how she dreads going to school because the people she sees in school were all a part of those lifetimes of degradation. I told her how she doesn't see how pretty she is and has trouble looking in the mirror. I told her how I know how she feels incredible pressure at trying to seem normal when she feels so empty and shameful inside.

I saw lifetimes that went deeper than the depraved lifetimes of sexual debauchery. I saw her being strapped down and locked up. I saw her in a straight jacket. I uncovered a secret that was causing her great inner conflict. I told her that I knew she felt like she was going crazy. But that was a reality bleeding through from the past. It was not her fate this life. She broke down in relief. I also called her on the pressure she was feeling to seem normal. In a past life, she was slightly off and it terrified her that she would be considered crazy because of it. She did end up being locked up in that lifetime. That was a huge concern bleeding through in this life.

"I release the pressure to appear normal; in all moments."

"I release the fear of being crazy; in all moments."

"I release feeling imprisoned; in all moments."

"I remove everything that is interfering with my Joy; in all moments."

Because of these kinds of lifetimes, people feel like they are unworthy. But there is always a core belief that is compelling the experiences that we have. In a past lifetime, she dabbled in the occult and gave her allegiance to the devil. After that, she felt damned. She created a string of lifetimes of depravity out of her guilt for her ingrained belief that she had sold her soul to the devil. We released all of those issues as well.

"I release selling my soul to the devil; in all moments."

As we went through the whole protocol with her and the devil, I felt her energy shift. Her physical appearance lightened. I told her that she was going to be able to see herself as pretty now. She dismissed me as if it wasn't possible. As we finished the taps, I was so excited to see her look in the mirror. What we were doing in the session was really resonating with her, but she couldn't think she could possibly see herself as pretty.

"Do you see how pretty you are?" I asked.

The Joy and light in her beautiful little face was priceless.

She took a moment..."Yes! I see it!"

We high-fived and hugged. We had just shifted the whole path of her life. She would now be able to feel her own joy and embrace the gifts that this lifetime held for her. She had prayed to be helped many lifetimes. Her prayers were answered. All the issues that she was holding in like a powder keg, were addressed, validated and explained. Finally, she can enjoy her innocence. It was a good session.

-Freedom Health Success-

Beauty and Self-Acceptance

When you embrace your own beauty in self-acceptance, you open up a portal to perpetual beauty for all. Doing so enhances your own sheen. When you loathe yourself or are self-derogatory in any way, you shut down all natural passageways to organic beauty.

-Joy Love Abundance

Where Beauty Dwells

Long fingernails are like high heels for your fingers. They render the energy current that runs through your body ineffective in connecting with other energy sources. These are ways that women are kept in a self-induced cage. Each strand of hair is like an antenna to our perceptions. Perhaps that is why it is systemically fashionable to thin it.

Bras do more than hold up the breasts. They are most likely made of synthetic fibers that shut down and suffocate the tissue underneath. Instead of wearing a pink ribbon to honor survivors, merely take off your bra. Not as a militant statement but for your wellbeing. Who dictated that breasts had to be firm to be attractive? Most likely some misogynist and no one questioned.

Why are only young women deemed attractive? Sure, there is a special glow in a child whose body has developed into maturity. It is like the light of a child emanating through the body of an adult. This one fleeting moment in a life is what people are trying to recapture, emulate and bed down. It is a form of touching heaven.

Yet it is not recaptured by mutilating the body, self-loathing, starving or torturing the body in any way. No "fits" of wanting, desperation or jealously can tap into that state again. It is entered effortlessly through the pure state of kindness and self-acceptance. These two things combined are the magic bullet for inner beauty to reemerge. You don't see an infomercial to sell that ware though.

You want to be beautiful? Love yourself. Talk to every part of your body and tell it how beautiful it is. That is what Gina Lollobrigida would do as a beauty practice. It must have fallen on deaf ears.

It doesn't serve women to attack the goal of being beautiful like male energy would do. That is, make it a goal to compete with other women, use beauty as a weapon and put on their female garb like a soldier going to battle.

Female energy embraces the atmosphere of sisterhood. It is happy to see others as beautiful and encourages other women effortlessly. Female energy is not self-conscious and can toss her hair around as freely as nature tosses around leaves. She is a deep connection to nature through loving all living things as if they have emerged from her own body, because they have.

Every woman is a manifestation and a portal to the magical ways of nature if she allows herself to be. In her more natural state, she is a personification of Goddess energy. She uses her stance of beauty not to conquer every male through sexual prowess but by loving every being as a dear one. This enhances her beauty.

If you want the world to respect nature again, embrace the beauty of yourself as an extension of nature. Through this way, beauty will reemerge in you, in the appreciation of nature and in the world. When you embrace your own beauty in self-acceptance, you open up a portal to perpetual beauty for all. Doing so enhances your own sheen. When you loathe yourself or are self-derogatory in any way, you shut down all natural passageways to organic beauty.

-Freedom Health Success-

Woman's Exponential Beauty

There is a commercial that irritates me a bit, and I have been wondering why. It is a few average-sized women in their underwear being interviewed on how to wear deodorant. It just irritates me, and it does a disservice to women (besides the obvious reason that most deodorants are so unhealthy for the body).

The message of the campaign is to say that women are beautiful in all body types. I understand. But the concept that women have to be half-naked and mocked up to be coy or cutesy is offensive. This seems more obvious in regular body-typed women for some reason. Probably because a woman's exponential beauty is magnified when she is conveying an outer form that is not pandering to an intangible outer sense of approval of discerning eyes.

Maybe the whole point of a society using such lithe half-naked women is not because they are more desirable in themselves. Maybe they are hiding a more insidious fantasy. Perhaps the stereotypical version of sexy women is closer to the illusion of being childlike in their body type and coy demeanor.

Maybe it taps into the taboo of wanting to be with a child merely blooming into womanhood.

Perhaps men being attracted to women who depict extreme youth shows their inadequacies as men who are reminiscing about a time in their youth when they were discovering the new romp of their own testosterone. Perhaps women desperately trying to be young and attractive for men is so men can overcompensate for their own nostalgia of that fleeting moment into manhood. If so, this desire in men reveals more about themselves than it does to diminish women.

Perhaps the commercial was exaggerating the fact that the image of beauty is bottlenecked into only being valid if it induces sexual arousal. Female beauty expresses itself in so many organic ways that it is offensive to seeing it pigeonholed into only being valid if is stimulates a man to arousal.

For me, seeing half-naked women being interviewed for how they use deodorant objectifies them in a way that is distasteful. It seems beneath them. It feels like they are being treated like performing monkeys. Perhaps all women have been treated like preforming monkeys, and I just didn't notice it behind my own admiration for the outer form. If this is what the commercial attempted to convey, then it was genius.

Personally, I believe that this society has run the whole sex and violence theme to the ground. When children are regularly getting gunned down in their schools by their peers, and schoolgirls are sold off for slavery merely for wanting an education, I think it is time to take responsibility for the imagery that we create.

Perhaps the world is in a state where uplifting imagery is more welcome. Perhaps creative people should use their talents to create instead of construct so many doomsday scenarios. Doing so does nothing to show gratitude for their talents. It just depicts a systemic self-loathing in the psyche that one is self -indulgently inflicting on the masses.

To me, there is nothing more beautiful than someone living their purpose. Whether it is a dancer with beautiful lines, a singer with an amazing heart, a mother with incredible patience, a service person with bravery and grit, or a vulnerable flawed individual speaking their truth, people in their angst for integrity and kindness are beautiful too. Who am I kidding? Everyone is beautiful to me. The world is drenched in beauty, perhaps more and more will be able to embrace it in its incredible range.

2: CASE STUDIES

Retrieving Your Energy from All Past Lovers

Recently I facilitated a private remote session with a woman who was trying to get over a breakup. It was her first session, so she was not used to how I work. As soon as I heard her voice, I could get a sense of her personal issues.

She was surprised at my first questions. I asked her what her relationship was with her father. I also asked if she cheated on her boyfriend. She told me that she was very close with her father, but he died when she was fifteen years old. She admitted that she did cheat on her boyfriend. They had been dating for four years, but she started to think about breaking up with him. There was no reason that she could name. The deep-seated reason was she was afraid that he would abandon her so she wanted to be in control by sabotaging the relationship before he had a chance.

When I tuned in, it didn't feel like they were done. I even got an impression of their two children. The problem was that she had lost his trust when she slept with someone else. On the surface it may seem like it is easy to just forgive the partner that you love when they have been with someone else. But from an energetic point of view, when one sleeps with someone other than their partner, they are actually stealing from their partner and giving that energy to another.

When two people come together in a love bond, they pool their energetic resources and both draw from the synergy of that pool. So when one strays to be with another, they are taking with them some of the energy that belongs to their partner. For her to have a chance to get back with her boyfriend, we had to retrieve her boyfriend's energy from the person she slept with and return it to him to make him whole.

Here are the taps that I led her through. There was no judgment involved. It is just the phrasing that came through to penetrate her walls. She broke down in doing the very first tap. That is a good sign that she was receptive to the shift. Instead of being offended, she was grateful to being held accountable.

(Say each statement three times out loud while tapping on the top of your head at the crown chakra and say it a fourth time while tapping on your chest at the heart chakra.)

"I release being a manipulative bitch; in all moments."

"I release the fear and trauma of being abandoned; in all moments."

"I release the trauma of being betrayed; in all moments."

"I release betraying my love; in all moments."

"I recant all vows and agreements between myself and all

past lovers; in all moments."

"I remove all curses between myself and all past lovers; in all moments."

"I remove all blessings between myself and all past lovers; in all moments."

"I sever all strings between myself and all past lovers; in all moments."

"I dissolve all karmic ties between myself and all past lovers; in all moments."

"I remove all the pain, burden, limitations, engrams and anger that all past lovers have put on me; in all moments."

"I remove all the pain, burden, limitations, engrams and anger that I have put on all past lovers; in all moments."

"I take back all the joy, love, abundance, freedom, health, success, security, companionship, creativity, peace, life, wholeness, beauty, enthusiasm, contentment, spirituality, enlightenment, and confidence that all past lovers have taken from me; in all moments."

"I give back all the joy, love, abundance, freedom, health, success, security, companionship, creativity, peace, life, wholeness, beauty, enthusiasm, contentment, spirituality, enlightenment, and confidence that I have taken from all past lovers; in all moments."

"I withdraw all my energy from all past lovers; in all

moments.”

"I release resonating with all past lovers; in all moments.”

"I release emanating with all past lovers; in all moments.”

"I remove all past lovers from my sound frequency; in all moments.”

"I remove all past lovers from my light body; in all moments.”

"I repair and fortify the Wei Chi of all my bodies; in all moments.”

“I repair and fortify the Wei Chi of all past lovers that I have compromised; in all moments.”

"I shift my paradigm from all past lovers to joy, love abundance, freedom, health, success, security, companionship, creativity, peace, life, wholeness, beauty, enthusiasm, contentment, spirituality, enlightenment, and confidence; in all moments.”

"I transcend all past lovers; in all moments.”

"I am centered and empowered in Divine Love; in all moments.”

After her session, my client admitted that she was supposed to go on a date that night with a past lover. She then had no desire to go. She ended up canceling it

The Awakening of Awareness

Recently, I facilitated a first time remote session with someone who was a dynamic healer. But he didn't feel dynamic at all at the beginning of the call. I perceived something in him that I had never perceived in anyone before. His energy field seemed contained, but it was bruised on the outer layers of it. Energetically he looked like a perfectly contained circle that was very bruised like and old apple.

He told me he was a substitute teacher. WHAT? This is the last job a sensitive soul should be doing. Children in a group can be very ruthless with infinite energy. Why was he subjecting himself to this kind of abuse? He thought it was income related. But nothing is. We set up the conditions in our lives and then pretend to be the victim of them. This is what he was doing by being a teacher while having such sensitivities.

A lifetime that was relevant opened up to show how he was creating this dynamic. In a past life he was an explorer who rejected convention to explore the wilderness. He became very isolated and almost didn't survive until a community of Native Americans rescued him. But they did not know what to do with him.

They treated him like a captured animal and just ignored him. He was very confused and lonely. But then they realized that he could interact with them and they started to engage him more. As harsh as they were, their acceptance meant everything to him. They brutally abused him with merriment. This abuse translated in him as acceptance and a form of love.

In the present life, he was creating brutal conditions for himself to conjure up the degree of love and acceptance that he felt in that lifetime. They did eventually tie him up and slowly killed him. So that is what he has been experiencing in this life as well.

Another dynamic that he has been enjoying up until his session was a subtle disdain for female energy. I gave him the tap:

"I release hating female energy; in all moments."

It felt freeing to him. The interesting thing to note to any healer or maybe any professional is that they will no longer be able to achieve the success that they wish by doing it solely in male energy. They must embrace their female energy as well. As much as he was ready to share his healing gifts, because he was still doing it in male energy, he was having little success.

Past lifetimes came flooding through. He was a eunuch in a lifetime and really hated women for that lifetime. He was instrumental in diminishing female energy in the era that swept in the Dark Ages. He was loyal to male energy and that was showing up in his stubbornness in not giving up convention in this life. That was another motivation in being a schoolteacher when it clearly was not a good fit.

Here are some other taps I led him through:

(Say each statement three times while tapping on your head and say it a fourth time while tapping on your chest.)

"All curses of female energy are removed; all moments"

"All blessings of female energy are removed; in all moments."

"Desecration of female energy is released; in all moments."

"Rejection of female energy is eliminated; in all moments."

"All diminishing of female energy is released; in all moments."

"All blaming of female energy is released; in all moments."

"The balance of male and female energy is gratefully accepted; in all moments."

"All blockages to balanced male and female energy are removed; in all moments."

"The capacity to embrace the balance of male and female energy is expounded; in all moments."

The energy field of this man was healed, and he no longer felt bruised. As I released the sounds of his soul, gregarious laughter emerged from deep within. As his soul released the joy and gratitude for being freed, he sobbed on the other side of the call. It was a good first session.

I invited him to attend the group calls because they show dynamic healers how to be both empowered in male and female energy. There are very few examples. So many of those who are doing energy work these days are doing so in male energy. That is the limitation. When that limitation is removed, those who have been struggling will experience profound empowerment. This is true of all professions and all souls. This is what the awakening of awareness is all about. It is so exciting.

-Freedom Health Success-

The Problem with Women Today

This very important message came out in the private group session that I facilitated last night. It was an acerbic assessment of how women treat other women in society. Trying to be the prettiest, have the best clothes, steal one's boyfriend, gossip about or belittle another woman is not female energy. It is a woman doing male energy in the female form. It is vulgar and a desecration of the sisterhood of Goddess energy.

Even the subtle means of wanting to outshine another woman is an indication that there is too much male energy at play. It is male energy that is single pointed with only one clear victor and an enjoyment of besting their friends for sport. This is a part of their strength and internal wiring, but it is not so charming in women.

Female energy wants everyone to be empowered. Female energy enhances the beauty of all by seeing them in such light. Female energy honors her Goddess sisters by embracing the highest possible manifestation of them in every way. To do less is to desecrate Goddess energy and to diminish one's own glow.

It may be thought okay to say that, "everybody does it, and so it is okay," but no. You as a Goddess are better than that. You know who you are and you see how beautiful I see you. I honor the Goddess in you by holding you accountable for your actions and how you serve Gaia in this way.

At one time, a sister Goddess would never speak or even think harshly about a fellow sister Goddess. If a woman continues to do this, it is a statement that she is in agreement with male energy's belief that it's superior. We all are Goddess energy. Let's start acting the reverent part we are meant to play. Let's hold ourselves to a higher standard so that all female energy can empower itself in human form.

We have the ability, awareness, capability and the responsibility to do this. You can sense the truth of this and hopefully correct this issue with yourself and your friendships. You are not as invisible as you may believe. You are watched and encouraged every step of the way. You know the truth of it and it is time to come into total alignment with truth.

-Joy Love Abundance-

The Second Session

I don't remember all my clients. There is so much information flowing through that it seems impossible to keep track unless they come to me regularly. And even then, I sometimes have trouble. It varies from client to client. I have this regular client with which has become a running amusement.

As many sessions as she has done with me, I always just blank her out and have to ask if it is her first session with me. But as soon as I remember what occurred in one session, I remember everything. It is like I keep invisible notes on the session. Most clients don't mind and actually prefer this.

I was starting a session and had this client on the phone, and I asked her if she ever had a session with me. She had. In this session, she said that wanted to focus on her dynamics with her husband and child. I tried to remember her, so I asked what we had worked on before.

She told me the session was over three years ago. She had come to me because she wasn't having any periods at all, and it was a concern. But now she was coming to me and she had a child. I asked her what happened after her session.

She said her periods balanced out right after her session with me and she became pregnant soon after. I was thrilled for her but she was taking it all in stride. I remembered how drastic her situation when she had first called me was and how now, in hindsight, she didn't even give it a thought. I was happy and frustrated.

"Didn't you think I would have liked to know that you had such a blessed turn around?"

It had never even occurred to her. That is what happens when shifts happen. They are so natural and so complete that people don't even remember what distress they were in. It is like forgetting childbirth. In turn, they don't remember to give credit where it's due.

It is not important for the facilitator but for all those out there who are feeling the indelible mark of western ways when natural healing is so complete and much more uneventful.

-Freedom Health Success-

Release Being Drained of Your Energy

(Say each statement three times out loud while

continuously tapping on the top of your head at the crown chakra and say it a fourth time while tapping on your chest.)

"I release being drained of my energy; in all moments."

"I release giving up my life force willingly; in all moments."

"I release the belief that empowerment is futile; in all moments."

"I release being manipulated out of my energy; in all moments."

"I release exchanging my energy for a mere stroke of the ego; in all moments."

"I release giving up my energy to be in complacency; in all moments."

"I release choosing complacency over empowerment; in all moments."

"I dry up the connection between myself and all the sources that drain me; in all moments."

"I take back all my energy from all the sources that have drained me; in all moments."

"I release being susceptible to those who feed off me; in all moments."

"I release giving away my energy; in all moments."

"I release martyring myself; in all moments."

"I strip all illusion off of all sources that drain energy; in all moments."

"I release being a helpless muse; in all moments."

"I shift my paradigm from being a helpless muse to being empowered and aware; in all moments."

"I am centered and empowered in being empowered and aware; in all moments."

-Joy Love Abundance-

Peeling off Layers

I just finished facilitating a first time session with someone who heard me on the local radio show. She was very perceptive in energy but she so wanted to let me know how aware she was. I knew. I could tell right away. But because of all the groups she attended where they wanted to be superior, she was trying to prove how aware she was. I actually had to remind her of times in history when we worked together as friends and equals. That seemed to validate her and allow her to work with me in the session. Before that, she was fighting every tap. She explained later that it was like there were two dynamics at play within her. One was really excited about doing the work. The other was like a tired child who just wanted to go to sleep.

Here are the taps I led her through exactly in the order I gave them to her. They seem very random, but they peeled off a layer at a time. They resonated as very helpful to her, and she could feel stagnant energy releasing. I had no outer information on her, and she was amazed at the shifts she experienced.

This was her first experience doing tapping. She now holds the key to releasing all her layers without having to give her power over to anyone ever again.

(Say each statement three times while tapping on your head and say it a fourth time while tapping on your chest.)

"I release being overlooked; in all moments."

"I release looking for God in validation; in all moments."

"I release the exhaustion of trying; in all moments."

"I release the belief that God hates me; in all moments."

"I release the belief that God is punishing me; in all moments."

"I release feeling abandoned by God; in all moments."

"I release the fear of being separated from my consciousness; in all moments."

"I release sabotaging myself and blaming God; in all moments."

"I release carrying the shame of the invalidation of female energy; in all moments."

"I release playing the victim; in all moments."

"I release my part in diminishing female energy; in all moments."

"I release being entrenched in male energy; in all moments."

"I release the trauma of being raped; in all moments."

"I release being manhandled; in all moments."

"I nullify all contracts with the rapist; in all moments."

"I remove all that was shoved into me by the rapist; in all moments."

"I take back all that the rapist has taken from me; in all moments."

"I dissolve all constructs with the rapist; in all moments."

"I regain my calm; in all moments."

"I release the guilt and trauma of having a miscarriage; in all moments."

"I release being a control freak; in all moments."

"I release being a know-it-all; in all moments."

"I release saying f@%& you to Jen; in all moments."

"I release one-upping Jen; in all moments."

"I flush out all the pain and trauma that is stored in my beingness; in all moments."

"I release the belief that I am less than whole; in all moments."

"I release being enslaved to Catholicism; in all moments."

"I nullify all contracts with a manmade god; in all moments."

"I recant all vows and agreements made to a manmade god; in all moments."

"I release the need to prove my worth; in all moments."

"I regain self-respect; in all moments."

"I awaken to potential; in all moments."

"I release wasting energy on one upping others; in all moments."

"I release fighting the world; in all moments."

"I melt my own walls from within; in all moments."

"I am centered and empowered in divine love; in all moments."

"I give myself permission to know myself energetically; in all moments."

Free Yourself of Others' Intentions

"I release allowing anyone from overlaying their intentions for myself or my life over my own; in all moments."

"I release allowing any group from overlaying their intentions for myself or my life over my own; in all moments.

"I release allowing anyone from overlaying their intentions for my body over my own; in all moments."

"I release allowing any group from overlaying their intentions for my body over my own; in all moments."

"I release allowing anyone from overriding my intentions for myself or my life with theirs; in all moments."

"I release allowing any group from overriding my intentions for myself or my life with their own; in all moments."

"I release allowing anyone from overriding my intentions for my body with their intentions for my body; in all moments."

"I release allowing any group from overriding my intentions for my body with their intentions for my body; in all moments."

"I release allowing anyone to railroad my intention for my body or life; in all moments."

"I release allowing any group to railroad my intention for my body or life; in all moments."

"I release allowing anyone from railroading my intentions for my body with their own; in all moments."

"I release allowing any group from railroading my intentions for my body with their own; in all moments."

-Joy Love Abundance-

Empowering the Yin

All our relationships that we play out in this world are a reflection of the dynamics of what plays out within ourselves. If you want to fix your relationships in the world, fix the dynamics within yourself. A man who doesn't respect women is more apt to disregard the yin of his own energetic makeup. A woman who is a go-getter yet secretly has self-esteem issues may also be disregarding her own yin.

The male and female energy, or the yin and yang of each person, need to be balanced. Balance within reflects in balance within all. This is the moment to get this right. We are not rogues in a kamikaze through life. We are empowered individuals giving voice and purpose to all others through our advancement in self-value.

"All patronization of female energy is released; in all moments."

"All placating of female energy is released; in all moments."

"All minimizing of female energy is released; in all moments."

"All of subjugating female energy is released; in all moments."

"All exploitation of female energy is released; in all moments."

"All domination of female energy is released; in all moments."

"All proving of points to female energy is released; in all moments."

"All imbalances between male and female energy are released; in all moments."

"All demi-godding in male energy is released; in all moments."

"All facades of male and female energy are released; in all moments."

Empowering Female Energy

As I facilitate sessions with many people, I see some recurring themes show up in their past lives. There are many lifetimes when women were diminished and defiled. It is not only a female issue. I see it show up in most people's Akashic records.

Throughout history, women have been defiled and seen as inferior. This still plays out around the world in women not being allowed the same freedoms as men. It is mind boggling for those in cultures with more freedom that women are being denied simple human rights. Yet it plays out in America as well in more subtle forms of discrimination.

This imbalance between male energy and female energy in the world affects us all. It shows up as incredible abuse of power, lack of compassion and inequality between men and women on the most subtle levels. The good news is that more people are becoming savvy to the direct connection between the individual and the whole. The more that individuals release their lifetimes of programming that men are superior, the more the whole can indeed come into balance.

We have all been men. We have all diminished women. We have all added our energies to the condition the world is in today. Here is a way energetically to undo what we have all contributed to. These taps are for all men and women to do to assist in helping the dynamics in the world balance out. We can help the world by doing these taps as surrogates for those who have abused and those who have been abused. By doing these taps, we will be assisting the world in drawing more upon the strengths of the female energy in the world.

"I release the belief that women are evil; in all moments."

"I release the belief that women are whores; in all moments."

"I release the belief that women are weak; in all moments."

"I release hating women; in all moments."

"I release diminishing women; in all moments."

"I release raping women; in all moments."

"I release the trauma of being raped; in all moments."

"I release beating women; in all moments."

"I release killing women; in all moments."

"I release the trauma of childbirth; in all moments."

"I release robbing the womb; in all moments."

"I release the trauma of having my baby ripped from my womb; in all moments."

"I release the belief that women are inferior to men; in all moments."

"I release the belief that men are superior to women; in all

moments."

"I release stealing women's gifts; in all moments."

"I release enslaving women; in all moments."

"I recant all vows and agreements between myself and female energy; in all moments."

"I remove all curses between myself and female energy; in all moments."

"I dissolve all diminishing views about women; in all moments."

"I remove all negative programming in regards to women; in all moments."

"I dissolve all karmic ties between myself and female energy; in all moments."

"I remove all the pain, burden and limitations that being female has put on me; in all moments."

"I remove all the pain, burden and limitations that I have put on all women; in all moments."

"I take back all the joy, love, abundance, freedom, health, success, security, companionship, creativity, peace, life, wholeness and balance that being female has taken from me; in all moments."

"I give back all the joy, love, abundance, freedom, health, success, security, companionship, creativity, peace, life, wholeness and balance that I have taken from all women; in all moments."

"I release defining being female as inferior; in all moments."

"I empower female energy; in all moments."

"I release the power struggle between women and men; in all moments."

"I balance out the yin and yang; in all moments."

"I am centered in equality between women and men; in all moments."

"I define women as the joy, love, abundance, freedom, health, success, security, companionship, creativity, peace, life, wholeness and balance; in all moments."

"I make space in this world for empowered, valued female energy equal to male energy; in all moments."

"I remove all blockages to having empowered, valued female energy equal to male's in the world; in all moments."

"I stretch the world's capacity to accept empowered, valued female energy equal to male's in the world; in all moments."

3: MALE-FEMALE DYNAMICS

Undoing the Abuse of Male Energy in the World

Recently in a contemplation, I was shown many different strong men. One was on crutches and screaming for someone to meet him. The teen boy was just watching the behavior. There was another man in the house afraid to go outside. He was hiding from the other man. This is what I understood from the imagery.

They were all healthy men. The one in the car was using his strength as a crutch to get his own way instead of to empower anything, including himself. The teenage boy was observing how to be a man by watching. He was learning the wrong lesson. The man in the house was strong and whole, but he was afraid of his own strength. He thought himself weak. That made him weak.

It occurred to me from this that I have never posted taps to assist the male energy in correcting itself. Here is my attempt. You do not need to be male to do these. We all have a component of both Yin and Yang in us. May this help bring those in balance for the individuals and the collective.

"I release using male energy as a crutch; in all moments."

"I release the belief that men are entitled; in all moments."

"I release the belief that men are better than women; in all

moments."

"I release abusing male energy; in all moments."

"I release the fear of my own power; in all moments."

"I release the fear, guilt and trauma of abusing power; in all moments."

"I release using male energy to dominate female; in all moments."

"I release hiding behind male energy; in all moments."

"I recant all vows and agreements between myself and male energy; in all moments."

"I release all imbalances between male and female; in all moments."

"I heal the bastardization of female energy; in all moments."

"I remove all curses between myself and male energy; in all moments."

"I remove all blessings between myself and male energy; in all moments."

"I dissolve all karmic ties between myself and male energy; in all moments."

"I release defining male energy as an abuse of power; in all moments."

"I remove all the pain, burden and limitations that male energy has put on female energy; in all moments."

"I return to female energy all the Joy, Love, Abundance, Freedom, Life and Wholeness that male energy has taken from it; in all moments."

"I shift my paradigm from male domination to an equal balance between male and female; in all moments."

"I empower the female to stand equal with the male; in all moments."

"I am centered and empowered by an equality of importance between the male and female energy; in all moments."

"I make space in this world for the equal balance of male and female energies; in all moments."

"I remove all blockages to having an equal balance of male and female energies in this world; in all moments."

"I stretch the world's capacity to accept and embrace an equal balance of male and female energies in this world; in all moments."

The human brain and heart, working together to manifest to its greatest capacity, have never been tested. We have cowered in a corner of our own psyche for way too long. Here is to testing our abilities and creating a confidence in ourselves far beyond what we ever have imagined. This is the time to do it. This is the time to pull each other out of the sludge of apathy and indifference and purify ourselves in the emanations of a new enlightenment. This is the moment of now.

-Joy Love Abundance-

Energetic Divorce

Have you ever wondered why it isn't that easy to end a relationship that has run its course? You make each other miserable perhaps, but you can't bring yourselves to separate from each other. Maybe it is because you have been together many lifetimes. Maybe that initial impulse when you first met wasn't kismet but a recognition of someone you have known very intimately in a past era.

Maybe the reason your partner always seemed to know you so well is because they really do know you so well. Maybe they have had lifetimes to study you. But that doesn't mean that you were meant to be together. Maybe this is the life that you are meant to finally end a relationship that has been following you through the ages. Maybe you are strong enough to end it now and are ready for another adventure.

In past lifetimes, maybe you have made vows to your current mate that you will be devoted to them forever. Maybe the devotion you presently show them, you had actually made in another time. Maybe you vowed to love them forever. So possibly, it isn't love that brought you together but an antiquated agreement made in a simpler time. That "I will love you forever," that was said many lifetimes ago, may still have some sticking power. Maybe it needs to be unglued from both of your energy fields. Maybe you can do you both a favor by unsticking you both from an old agreement.

Maybe you both cursed each other. A curse is merely an intention that is nailed into reality with passion. It can be as simple as saying, "You will never love anyone as much as you love me." Or, "You will be miserable without me." Maybe you both are not so in love or meant to be together. Maybe you both are merely walking through the curses that you have both put on each other.

When two people are intimate, they share all their resources. It is like their energy goes into a communal pool of which both partake. But when you break up and separate, each person takes a part of the joined energy. You take some of theirs; they take some of yours. When you meet again in another lifetime and are drawn to this stranger, it may be because you are seeing your own energy in them. No wonder you were so drawn to this person, you were seeing a missing piece of yourself in them.

These taps were given to me from my Spirit Guides as a protocol to undo the energetic entanglement that we have done to each other. When a couple breaks up, they return all their possessions to each other. This protocol is doing the same thing energetically. It is the layman given the tool to untangle the energetic mess that they have wrapped themselves in with another person. There is no need to give your power away ever again. Now you have the perfect tool.

There are couples that don't know if they are meant to be together or not. The beauty of doing these taps is, if you are really meant to be together, doing these taps will just clean the slate and recalibrate a relationship. If you are meant to stay together, you will stay together.

This protocol is simply meant to put your fate back in your own hands where it should be. It is not merely words. Doing this protocol is you being the shaman; it is you being empowered. It is you taking back your energy and releasing the things that have been weighing you down. It is also repairing your energy field so that you are not susceptible in the future.

It may feel so freeing to do these taps in regard to your partner that you may want to do them regarding every person in your life. You may want to untangle yourself from every family member, co-worker, boss and friend. You may even want to do this protocol with every organization or idea that has held you back. Here is to you freeing yourself in a very profound way. Maybe in releasing all entanglements, you can finally get an understanding of who you really are unhindered and free.

(Say each statement three times out loud while continuously tapping on the top of your head at the crown chakra, and say it a fourth time while tapping on your chest at the heart chakra.)

"I release being with ___________ out of habit; in all moments."

"I release feeling dependent on ____________; in all moments."

"I release feeling beholden to ___________; in all moments."

"I release being enslaved to ___________; in all moments."

"I remove all vivaxes between myself and _____________; in all moments."

"I remove all tentacles between myself and _____________; in all moments."

"I recant all vows and agreements between myself and ___________; in all moments."

"I remove all curses between myself and __________; in all moments."

"I remove all blessings between myself and __________; in all moments."

"I sever all strings and cords between myself and __________; in all moments."

"I dissolve all karmic ties between myself and __________; in all moments."

"I remove all the pain, burden, limitations and engrams

that _________ has put on me; in all moments."

"I remove all the pain, burden, limitations and engrams that I have put on ___________; in all moments."

"I take back all the joy, love, abundance, freedom, health, success, security, companionship, creativity, peace, life, wholeness, beauty, enthusiasm, contentment, spirituality, enlightenment and confidence that ____________ has taken from me; in all moments."

"I give back all that I have taken from ____________; in all moments."

"I withdraw all my energy from ____________; in all moments."

"I release resonating with ______________; in all moments."

"I release emanating with ______________; in all moments."

"I remove all of _____________ from my sound frequency; in all moments."

"I remove all of _____________ from my light body; in all moments."

"I shift my paradigm from __________ to joy, love, abundance, freedom, health, success, security, companionship, creativity, peace, life, wholeness, beauty, enthusiasm, contentment, spirituality, enlightenment and confidence; in all moments."

"I strip all illusion off of ___________; in all moments."

"I transcend ____________; in all moments."

"I repair and fortify the Wei Chi on all my bodies; in all moments."

"I align all my bodies; in all moments."

"I am centered and empowered in divine love and peace; in all moments."

"I make space in this world to know love and peace: in all moments."

"I remove all blockages to knowing love and peace; in all moments."

"I stretch my capacity to recognize love and peace; in all moments."

"I stretch my capacity to embrace love and peace; in all moments."

-Freedom Health Success-

The Empowerment of All

It is a lie that those in a female body can't reach the

spiritual heights that male energy can attain. This belief is a half-truth that keeps some souls trapped at a certain level. This belief keeps humanity in apathy. At a certain level of awareness, an individual can manipulate the molecular makeup of their atoms to achieve whatever intention is their spiritual purpose.

If you are on a spiritual path, you owe it to yourself to challenge everything that you have ever been told. Everything. If you are not doing this, then you have deduced the intention of your spiritual journey into a dead form of worship.

The vibrations of this world are presently more conducive to female energy realizing its worth much more than it ever has been in recorded history. Female energy, as loving and confident as it is, simply cannot take a backseat to male energy in any form. Converting its benevolent nature into a passive state has been a detriment to humanity.

If female energy is empowered, she must stand toe to toe with male energy. This does not mean being confrontational. It just means not deferring either. The fantasy of finding the perfect man to take care of you is a seed desire planted into female energy to divert it off course. If female energy desires male energy, it may likely be that she is craving to marry her own empowerment and give presence to the submerged male energy within her own beingness.

No longer is it necessary to sit at the feet of anyone. Every individual has the means and tools to attain Mastership.

Waiting around for male energy to give permission, say the right thing to induce enlightenment, or "allow" one to transcend, is a futile act.

Mastership is not achieving a gold star or prized ribbon. It is digging in the dirt of fertile experiences with your own hands and sowing your own seeds. Spirituality is not a commune. It is an extremely personalized journey that demands that you drop all beliefs, crutches and facades to gain your greatest empowerment. In doing so, all individuals and all of humanity are elevated to sublime heights.

In a way, the heavens are drying up from lack of our attention. The power mongers have nearly succeeded in making access nearly impossible. It is important to feed the creative well of imagination. The imagination is the precipice of greater awareness and the enlightenment of humanity.

Dreams are an active piece of participating in the more subtle realms. Why are such things demonized or trivialized? Because they throw a wrench into the plans of those who wish to enslave humanity. Why do people resent me so much? Because the parts of them that are gripped by power are whispering in their ear that I am the enemy.

If someone has not achieved the heights that they desire in their present belief system, perhaps there is a flaw in the belief system and not themselves. Any person or group that instills fear for wanting more truth is violating spiritual law. Anyone who instills fear in another, no matter how subtle, is pulling one away from the love because fear is the opposite of love.

None will know what I endure to share such truth. One has to ask, why? There is no benefit to myself in spending up to fifteen hours a day writing and assisting others. I have no personal agenda. In all my writings, I have shared nothing about any ego gratification in doing what I do. The satisfaction I receive is in assisting others from having to endure a struggle equal in intensity to my own.

My only motive is in sharing truth and to advocate for self-empowerment and healing. If one resents me, and many do, they may want to look at their own belief system and see what is lacking that makes them insecure about the truth I share. Perhaps they resent their own path for not providing the pathway to truth that I do. I am not creating a group of any kind. I am not trying to get people to leave their group. I am merely doing what love and my Guides compel me to do.

I appreciate any kindness offered, that's true. But it is solely used for fuel to propel my intention farther so all of humanity can awaken to its empowerment. I convert all loving intentions into healing energy and send it out into the world. My imagination allows me access to such wonderment, healing abilities and empowerment. And so does yours.

I simply love.

Transgender

We have all been both male and female. In my sessions with clients, I see their past lives and what they have endured. I see rapes, tortures, manipulations, babies delivered and stolen from the womb, being sacrificed, forced to marry, being passed around, imprisonment, wars, murders, killing of babies, abuses of power and violations and degradations that are unimaginable.

In some people, the abuse has been devastating. Some have suffered more abuse as a woman and others, more abuse as a man. It is natural to avoid that which brings us pain. But as soul, we still have to collect our experiences.

How does one collect their experiences as a woman if they are terrified of the lifetimes that they have endured in a female body? How does one choose to come into a female body if they have been raped, violated, mutilated and desecrated beyond all reason every time they have? Some may choose to get their female experiences in the safety of a male body, others vice versa.

For some people, it is a miracle that they can even choose to incarnate, interact with others and still have a capacity to love. It is just too much to ask that they blend with the herd. It is a ridiculous request. If all the cards were laid on the table, and everyone could see all the lifetimes of others, there would be no more judgment. There would just be humble resolve and respect. We would all go out of our way to serve others because we have compassion for what they have endured. We would feel like idiots for judging anything about them, as well we should.

This is a great day to honor the unique path of others and so is every day. Celebrate their kindness, uniqueness and resilience. Honor their ability to thrive. Show gratitude and respect for the life they have forged for themselves. Admire their differences and what they reveal to you about yourself. This is how we evolve as individuals, and as a species.

-Freedom Health Success-

The Yin and Yang of Male Energy

Since female energy has been stripped from our repertoire, women have been forced to be women in male energy. Since male energy wants to do all the yang aspects of male energy, (winning, being the best, being adulated), all that is left for female energy to thrive in is the yin of male energy. These are not the most desired qualities.

But once we start to put value on female qualities like creativity, compassion, imagination, honoring the earth and valuing all, there will be a vast shift in consciousness. All souls, except the most ruthless barbarians, are hungry for this shift.

The Unconscious Memory of the Stripper

I have facilitated a handful of sessions for different exotic dancers. None of them felt shame in dancing. In fact, it was spiritual for some and a means of connecting with something greater. What I have experienced is that dancing may be a way to preserve an ancient ritual of worship. Tuning into a few of them, I was able to piece together an ancient history.

In ancient times, man was not considered superior to woman. They both were known for different strengths. While man seemed to focus all his energy on an objective goal and "target" it, woman was able to "relax" her energy field so it encompassed all. She would "sense" all the subtleties that were lost on man.

Lands were ruled with great wisdom and compassion. Women were groomed in great lineages just as men were as kings. The most wise and gifted seers were groomed to be wed to their male counterpart. There were temples to teach women the intuitive arts and the greatest priestesses were wed to the greatest kings. These were the most successful sovereignties.

Barbarians grew jealous of the wealth of the great kingdoms. They were not strong enough or smart enough to battle the kings. So they destroyed the wisdom schools that women were trained in. They raided and desecrated the temples, raped the women and scattered them to the ignorant. They forced them to wed to improve their status.

When they still lacked the success they desired, they grew angrier with the women for withholding their gifts. They used the women as showpieces for their conquest. They forced them to perform their rituals as a way to show off their skills and retell the tale of their conquest. Women would go through the motions with the rituals, which became a form of dance.

The priestesses desperately missed their homelands. They were isolated and defeated. When they danced for the barbarians, it was a way to stay connected to their sisters and was their plea to God to rescue them. For man, the dance symbolized his conquest of her. Without an understanding of her gifts, and her without physical strength, he deemed her weak and useless. She became a showpiece for a conquest and not much more to him.

In the generations to follow, the women tried to remember the ways of the seer and pass them down to their daughters. But they were not able to preserve technique or purpose behind the dance. It became a means to pacify their mates. The subtle arts were lost and replaced with the art of seduction.

Many exotic dancers hold the memory of these ancient ways and are attempting to connect with a greater aspect of themselves through stripping. Maybe the men who attend the strip clubs are also remembering an ancient time of the conquest.

-Freedom Health Success-

Technique to Bring Internal and External Balance

"I release valuing yang over yin; in all moments."

It may create a sense of being more grounded (which is the way the mind may process more balance), right away.

-Joy Love Abundance-

Stop "Yanging" up Your Yin

There are so many people looking for love. Does it need to be so difficult? A recent session revealed a couple of issues preventing a woman from attracting a mate. It has always been obvious to me that many women who wear makeup and a power wardrobe to attract a man are doing so in male energy. It is as if they are putting on their war paint when they go out clubbing.

Recently a client revealed two of her past lives that were interfering with her attracting a mate. One of them was a life as a Geisha. In that life, she was trained to be very submissive to men. It left her feeling vulnerable as a woman. But even more damaging to her was interpreting being female as a negative, passive experience.

From this experience and others, she defined her yin

energy as passive. Being in yin energy came to feel like a very vulnerable state to her. She avoided it as much as possible. As a result, she stayed in yang energy most of the time. Even when she was interested in a man, unbeknownst to her, when she liked someone, she was engaging him in male energy. Her yang energy trying to attract a yang male would just not work. It had nothing to do with her being pretty or worthy enough. It was just a simple matter of the Law of Attraction. Yang energy will repel yang energy every time.

Another lifetime was getting in the way of her attracting a mate as well. There was a past lifetime where she was a gay male soldier. She was in love with another soldier who was her soul mate. He was not gay. He would have been repulsed at the thought of a romantic relationship with another man. Knowing this, the gay soldier made certain to always be a good friend to him. As painful as it was, he preferred to suffer in silence rather than risk losing a connection with the love of his life. That lifetime of innate rejection was bleeding through to this life.

Our natural state is joy, so the more devastating an experience is, the greater it contrasts our natural state. It is then ingrained more deeply into our Akashic records. When the woman met someone she was attracted to, she naturally went into friend mode as it was ingrained from that past experience. This woman was trying to attract a man using passive yang energy. It was still yang energy. No matter what, yang will always repel yang regardless of whether it is in a yin body or not.

Here is why the taps are so important. Trying to rectify this would take a lot of therapy even if it were possible. Here are the taps that we used to correct this at a deep level. The shift was immediate as we could both feel it and hear it in her voice.

"I release diminishing my yin; in all moments."

"I release the belief that yin is weak; in all moments."

"I release the fear of being yin; in all moments."

"I release feeling vulnerable in yin; in all moments."

"I release confusing yin with being geisha; in all moments."

"I remove all negative engrams of being geisha; in all moments."

"I release habitually diminishing my yin; in all moments."

"I release making my yin inoperable; in all moments."

"I release being enslaved to diminishing my yin; in all moments."

"I repair and fortify the Wei Chi of my yin; in all moments."

"I remove all engrams of diminished yin from my beingness; in all moments."

"I remove all vivaxes between myself and diminishing my yin; in all moments."

"I remove all tentacles between myself and diminishing my yin; in all moments."

"I remove the claws of diminishing my yin from my beingness; in all moments."

"I recant all vows and agreements between myself and diminishing my yin; in all moments."

"I remove all curses between myself and diminishing my yin; in all moments."

"I remove all blessings between myself and diminishing my yin; in all moments."

"I sever all strings and cords between myself and diminishing my yin; in all moments."

"I dissolve all karmic ties between myself and diminishing my yin; in all moments."

"I remove all the pain, burden, limitations and confusion that diminishing my yin has put on me; in all moments."

"I remove all the pain, burden, limitations and confusion that me diminishing my yin has put on my partner; in all moments."

"I take back all that diminishing my yin has taken from me; in all moments."

"I give back to my partner all that me diminishing my yin has taken from them; in all moments."

"I release resonating with diminishing my yin; in all moments."

"I release emanating with diminishing my yin; in all moments."

"I extract all of diminishing my yin from my sound frequency; in all moments."

"I extract all of diminishing my yin from my light emanation; in all moments."

"I shift my paradigm from diminishing my yin to having balanced yin and yang; in all moments."

"I transcend diminishing my yin; in all moments."

"I release overcompensating in yang; in all moments."

"I release always being in yang; in all moments."

"I release using a war cry to call forth love; in all moments."

"I release feeling safe only in yang; in all moments."

"I release confusing yang with being complete; in all moments."

"I release habitually overcompensating in yang; in all moments."

"I release making my yang the controlling faction; in all moments."

"I release being enslaved to overcompensating in yang; in all moments."

"I remove all masks, walls and armor from my yang; in all moments."

"I lay down my yang's sword and shield; in all moments."

"I remove all engrams of overcompensating in yang from my beingness; in all moments."

"I remove all vivaxes between myself and overcompensating in yang; in all moments."

"I remove all tentacles between myself and overcompensating in yang; in all moments."

"I remove the claws of overcompensating in yang from my beingness; in all moments."

"I recant all vows and agreements between myself and overcompensating in yang; in all moments."

"I remove all curses between myself and overcompensating in yang; in all moments."

"I remove all blessings between myself and overcompensating in yang; in all moments."

"I sever all strings and cords between myself and overcompensating in yang; in all moments."

"I dissolve all karmic ties between myself and overcompensating in yang; in all moments."

"I remove all the pain, burden, limitations and confusion that overcompensating in yang has put on me; in all moments."

"I remove all the pain, burden, limitations and confusion that me overcompensating in yang has put on my partner; in all moments."

"I take back all that overcompensating in yang has taken from me; in all moments."

"I give back to my partner all that me overcompensating in yang has taken from them; in all moments."

"I release resonating with overcompensating in yang; in all moments."

"I release emanating with overcompensating in yang; in all moments."

"I extract all of overcompensating in yang from my sound frequency; in all moments."

"I extract all of overcompensating in yang from my light emanation; in all moments."

"I shift my paradigm from overcompensating in yang to having balanced yin and yang; in all moments."

"I transcend overcompensating in yang; in all moments."

"I am centered and empowered in balanced yin and yang; in all moments."

"I resonate and emanate balanced yin and yang; in all moments."

-Freedom Health Success-

Release Male Slanted Truth

"I release giving my power to male slanted truth; in all moments."

"I release being at the mercy of male slanted truth; in all moments."

"I release being enslaved to male slanted truth; in all moments."

"I release using male slanted truth as a crutch; in all moments."

"I release subscribing to male slanted truth out of habit; in all moments."

"I release feeling dependent on male slanted truth; in all moments."

"I release feeling beholden to male slanted truth; in all moments."

"I release being brainwashed by male slanted truth; in all moments."

"I recant all vows and agreements between myself and male

slanted truth; in all moments."

"I remove all curses between myself and male slanted truth; in all moments."

"I remove all blessings between myself and male slanted truth; in all moments."

"I sever all strings and cords between myself and male slanted truth; in all moments."

"I dissolve all karmic ties between myself and male slanted truth; in all moments."

"I remove all the pain, burden, limitations and engrams that male slanted truth has put on me; in all moments."

"I remove all the pain, burden, limitations and engrams that I have put on all others due to male slanted truth; in all moments."

"I take back all the joy, love, abundance, freedom, health, success, security, companionship, creativity, peace, life, wholeness, beauty, enthusiasm, contentment, spirituality, enlightenment and confidence that male slanted truth has taken from me; in all moments."

"I give back all that I have taken from all others due to male slanted truth; in all moments."

"I withdraw all my energy from male slanted truth; in all moments."

"I release resonating with male slanted truth; in all

moments."

"I release emanating with male slanted truth; in all moments."

"I remove all of male slanted truth from my sound frequency; in all moments."

"I remove all of male slanted truth from my light body; in all moments."

"I shift my paradigm from male slanted truth to absolute truth; in all moments."

"I strip all illusion off of male slanted truth; in all moments."

"I transcend male slanted truth; in all moments."

"I repair and fortify the psyche of all my bodies; in all moments."

"I am centered and empowered in absolute truth; in all moments."

"I make space in this world for all to know absolute truth; in all moments."

"I remove all blockages to the world knowing absolute truth; in all moments."

"I stretch my capacity to recognize absolute truth; in all moments."

"I stretch my capacity to embrace absolute truth; in all moments."

"I resonate and emanate absolute truth; in all moments."

"I empower the world to resonate and emanate absolute truth; in all moments."

-Joy Love Abundance-

Release Male Issues

"I release being emasculated; in all moments."

"I release the schism; in all moments."

"I un-spiral our energies; in all moments."

"I release the trauma of having my survival threatened; in all moments."

"I release being stuck in male energy; in all moments."

"I release defending the behavior; in all moments."

"I break up the chunks; in all moments."

"I release condoning the abuse; in all moments."

"I release being a know-it-all; in all moments."

"I release deflecting; in all moments."

“I release the pain; in all moments.”

“I release being emotionally stunted; in all moments.”

“I release taking ownership of others; in all moments.”

“I release being an enabler; in all moments.”

“I release bragging; in all moments.”

“I release being a braggart; in all moments.”

“I release the bullshit anger; in all moments.”

“I release all the residual bullshit; in all moments.”

“I release selected deafness; in all moments.”

“I hear the love and beauty in all sounds; in all moments.”

“I release tolerating abuse; in all moments.”

-Freedom Health Success-

Release Desecrating Goddess

"I declare myself a surrogate for male energy in doing these taps; in all moments.”

"I release the belief that I am superior to women; in all moments.”

"I release raping women; in all moments."

"I release desecrating Goddess; in all moments."

"I release destroying my brethren; in all moments."

"I release subjugating Goddess; in all moments."

"I release subjugating myself by subjugating Goddess; in all moments."

"I release being obtuse; in all moments."

"I release being power-driven; in all moments."

"I release feeling threatened by women; in all moments."

"I release the belief that women are weak; in all moments."

"I release confusing honoring Goddess with being weak; in all moments."

"I release confusing being equal with women as being subjugated; in all moments."

"I release the perpetual need to prove myself; in all moments."

"I remove all vivaxes between myself and desecrating Goddess; in all moments."

"I remove all tentacles between myself and desecrating Goddess; in all moments."

"I remove the ugly claws of desecrating Goddess from my

beingness; in all moments.”

"I release being used to desecrate Goddess; in all moments.”

"I remove all programming and conditioning that desecrating Goddess has put on me; in all moments.”

"I remove all engrams of desecrating Goddess; in all moments.”

"I send all energy matrices into the light that desecrate Goddess; in all moments.”

"I command all complex energy matrices that desecrate Goddess to be escorted into the light by my guides; in all moments.”

"I nullify and void all contracts in desecrating Goddess; in all moments.”

"I recant all vows and agreements between myself and desecrating Goddess; in all moments.”

"I remove all curses between myself and desecrating Goddess; in all moments.”

"I remove all blessings between myself and desecrating Goddess; in all moments.”

"I nullify all payoffs in desecrating Goddess; in all moments.”

"I sever all strings, cords, and wires between myself and

desecrating Goddess; in all moments."

"I dissolve all karmic ties between myself and desecrating Goddess, in all moments."

"I strip all illusion off of desecrating Goddess; in all moments."

"I remove all masks, walls, and armor off of desecrating Goddess; in all moments."

"I collapse and annihilate desecrating Goddess; in all moments."

"I remove all the pain, burden, and limitations that desecrating Goddess has put on me; in all moments."

"I remove all the pain, burden, and limitations that desecrating Goddess has put on all others; in all moments."

"I remove all the pain, burden, and limitations that I have put on Goddess; in all moments."

"I remove all the fear, futility, and unworthiness that desecrating Goddess has put on me; in all moments."

"I remove all the fear, futility, and unworthiness that I have put on all others due to desecrating Goddess; in all moments."

"I remove all the fear, futility, and unworthiness that I have put on Goddess; in all moments."

"I remove all the illusion of separateness that has been put on me due to desecrating Goddess; in all moments."

"I remove all the illusion of separateness that I have put on all others due to desecrating Goddess; in all moments."

"I remove the illusion of separateness that I have put on Goddess; in all moments."

"I take back all that desecrating Goddess has taken from me; in all moments."

"I give back to all others, all that desecrating Goddess has taken from them; in all moments."

"I release resonating with desecrating Goddess; in all moments."

"I release emanating with desecrating Goddess; in all moments."

"I extract all of desecrating Goddess from my sound frequency; in all moments."

"I extract all of desecrating Goddess from the universal sound frequency; in all moments."

"I extract all desecrating Goddess from my light emanation; in all moments."

"I extract all of desecrating Goddess from the universal light emanation; in all moments."

"I shift my paradigm from desecrating Goddess to joy,

love, abundance, freedom, and wholeness; in all moments."

"I shift the universal paradigm from desecrating Goddess to joy, love, abundance, freedom, and wholeness; in all moments."

"I transcend desecrating Goddess; in all moments."

"I universally transcend desecrating Goddess; in all moments."

"I am centered and empowered in joy, love, abundance, freedom, and wholeness; in all moments."

"I am universally centered and empowered in joy, love, abundance, freedom, and wholeness; in all moments."

-Joy Love Abundance-

Permeating Properties of Female Energy

Last night, the Ancient Ones reminded me of the great ability of love to dissolve any attacks. Not in a Pollyanna way but as a solvent of all that is not pure. Even the most horrific psychic attacks respond to love. The love just melts them. Even things that seem as solid as steel.

Female energy is regaining its balance now in the worlds and the energy that has been predicated on male dominance will try to diminish female energy. But this is why you and I have incarnated into our particular form. We are not so attached to our loins but to the beautiful expansiveness that is female energy's nature.

We have chosen our forms to permeate the love into all the cracks and crevices male energy has overlooked even within its own nature. We are blessed for our standings in love. You know all this but a reminder is nice once in awhile.

-Joy Love Abundance-

The Marriage

Now is the time for female energy to take its rightful place next to male energy as empowering and purposeful. Female energy shall no longer see itself as servant, whore, or victim and will let go of the need to mimic the male gait.

-Freedom Health Success-

Dissipating a Male Dominated World

We are a compilation of both male and female energy. We cannot embrace and empower our female energy unless we beckon male energy to rescind its dominant grip on the psyche of the individual and society at large.

Male energy is fixated on the outcome. Female energy is immersed in the process, realizing that everything and everyone matters as well as the outcome. Male energy wants a competition in life even of the spiritual pursuit. Female energy wants everyone to prevail and to be the enlightened. It is the same energy that wants their children to succeed and be better than it. If anyone wants to diminish you for their own betterment, whether they are in a male body or female, that is the workings of an over healthy male energy. These taps assist to balance the male and female energy within all.

"I declare myself a surrogate for humanity in doing these taps; in all moments."

"I release the belief that men are superior to women; in all moments."

"I release the belief that women are weak; in all moments."

"I release preferring boys over girls; in all moments."

"I release condoning a male dominated world; in all moments."

"I release agreeing to a male dominated world; in all moments."

"I release being enslaved to a male dominated world; in all moments."

"I withdraw all my energy from a male dominated world; in all moments."

"I recant all vows and agreements between myself and a male dominated world; in all moments."

"I release squelching female energy; in all moments."

"I remove all curses between myself and a male dominated world; in all moments."

"I remove all blessings between myself and a male dominated world in all moments."

"I eradicate all imbalances that a male dominated world entails; in all moments."

"I remove all vivaxes between myself and a male dominated world; in all moments."

"I remove all tentacles that a male dominated world has in me; in all moments."

"I remove all tentacles that I have in a male dominated world; in all moments."

"I sever all strings and cords between myself and a male dominated world; in all moments."

"I dissolve all karmic ties between myself and a male dominated world; in all moments."

"I remove all the pain, burden, limitations and engrams that a male dominated world has put on me; in all

moments."

"I remove all the pain, burden, limitations and engrams that I have put on all others due to a male dominated world; in all moments."

"I take back all the joy, love, abundance, freedom, health, life, wholeness and balance that a male dominated world has taken from me; in all moments."

"I give back all the joy, love, abundance, freedom, health, life, wholeness and balance that I have taken from all others due to a male dominated world; in all moments."

"I release resonating with a male dominated world; in all moments."

"I release emanating with a male dominated world; in all moments."

"I extract all of a male dominated world from my sound frequency; in all moments."

"I extract all of a male dominated world from my light emanation; in all moments."

"I shift my paradigm from a male dominated world to a world of joy, love, abundance, freedom, health, life, wholeness and balance; in all moments."

"I transcend a male dominated world; in all moments."

"I am centered and empowered in a world of joy, love, abundance, freedom, health, life, wholeness and balance; in all moments."

Psychic Manipulation

This is how psychic manipulation works:

When we are asleep, we will get a subtle image pumped into us that supports an agenda. It is very similar to an energetic commercial. Once when I was watching a political convention, whose platform I did not necessarily agree with, a current of energy came to me in the night and tried to seduce me by kissing me on the lips. I then knew how otherwise loving compassionate people could be in agreement with such obviously unloving political stances. They were under the influence of a psychic manipulation.

I just experienced another one of these “commercials.” I have a dear friend and confidant. She is one of the very few people that I trust and has proven her loyalty and support to me again and again. After I was completing one dream scenario, credits started rolling as if it were the end of a movie. My dear friend's name was displayed on the screen and after that, appeared the words "is a liar." It was in a special font and everything.

I immediately knew that this was a psychic manipulation. I know this person's intention too well. But if I had any doubt, I would be suspect against my friend. It is so important for people to be savvy in energetic exchanges. All of politics is a demonstration in psychic manipulation. It is good to understand what is at stake.

It isn't just about an election. It’s about being wise to the ways of manipulation so that we can discern truth for ourselves. Most people have no idea what truth is and when I share it, people have a strong reaction to me. Maybe the dream was showing me what is being psychically thrown against me. Maybe that is why I get the negative reactions that I do.

Perhaps just showing you what is being done in the dream state on the astral realm will help some of you decipher truth for yourselves. That is the plan in sharing anyway. The truth that I share is new to the world. Of course, it is going to upset the status quo. Each person must gauge everything that comes into their orbit and discern the intention behind it. Who gains by your subscribing to something you are told?

In my case, all of humanity gains because I have been kept alive by a power greater than myself and put in a position to share truth. I have been destroyed and demonized many lifetimes to prevent me from assisting the individual gain spiritual freedom. But now is a golden window of opportunity. The gateways have been opened. The psychic ploys are so savvy that one really needs to want truth beyond all other outer trappings including security, clout, monetary gain and the stroking of the ego.

Truth is its own reward. If you believe this world is all there is, then stay on the path that society lays out for you. Celebrate the trivial victories. Gauge each thing you hear with the same credence, distract yourself with social events and wind this life down as the end of you as you know you. Or continue the journey into the other worlds confident and prepared. Lies don't dry up once you cross. You aren't instantly wise. One can be duped just as much on the astral plane as they are here. It is empowering to look for truth now and to consider the physical life as part of your journey into the higher realms. That is what spiritual freedom and enlightenment is all about. You will be able to thwart off all psychic influences merely by the purity of your own perception.

There was a part to the dream as well that is pertinent. There was a bridal couple on their wedding day. They were at the table at the reception. There were a few people observing them. I was there as an advisor. The groom did not know how to interact with his bride. They were both lit up and happy and were both gregarious people. But when the groom was pleased about how the event was going, he would turn to the facilitator of the wedding with his affection. It was funny to see him so clueless as to how to engage his new wife. He had no understanding of how to interact with her but was very good at interacting with the male facilitator of the wedding.

I immediately knew that this was depicting how clueless male energy is in engaging its counterpart. It is like there is no reference point. We are at the point in our evolutionary unfolding where male energy will blend with its female counterpart in all of us. I was directing the male from the other male and showing him how to engage his new wife. This is what I do in my writings. The reason I am in a female body is to empower the female energy to be the equal of its male counterpart. We are all taught to worship a male deity and that is the role that the facilitator played in the dream. The world has to turn away from the depiction of God being male and see it more as a neutral source that encompasses both male and female energy. How can women expect to be considered equal if they are still worshiping God depicted in a male body? This is one of those inconsistencies that get overlooked when we are taught not to question our faith.

Recently, I facilitated a private remote session with a woman who said that she does what I do. Immediately, I chided her because when you compare yourselves to another, you are doing it to piggyback on their abilities somehow. She understood that was what she was doing. She actually felt great shame when it came to me. She felt that she had wronged me on a very deep level. She had. She had wronged all of humanity.

In her session, it came to light that she started out from another planet that was at war with earth. She hated earth. She was sent here after her planet was destroyed and was expected to seed the primal earthlings with a more aware species. She resented being in this position. Being on earth after experiencing the freedom of other planets feels like being immersed in a sarcophagus. The human body is so restricting compared to bodies from other planets. When this happens, the individual romanticizes space. They appreciate the dark more than the light. They worship the dark. In this woman's instance, she was associating darkness with love. This permeated all of her earth lifetimes.

She is not alone. There are many who do this. There are

many who prefer the darkness because it represents the freedom of space for them. They may be the same ones who do not appreciate caring for earth. They see it as a disposable planet, using up its resources at an alarming rate. They have no love for earth. This is the shortsighted stance we see in those who are gutting the earth for monetary gain. But this woman's transgressions against earth ran deeper.

She wanted to keep the earth people trapped on earth. It was a plan to immerse them in ingrained ignorance, so they would not figure out their own empowerment as they evolved. They were taught to worship to dissipate their energy. Sending their energy up to the sky was one way to dissipate their energy. Putting steeples on all their holy buildings so the energy went out to space away from earth dissipated our own effectiveness. Even teaching them to aim their hands up into the sky when they prayed was another way to direct their energy away from their own empowerment. There was also something that the woman client was specifically responsible for.

She was the one who invented the clause that is in every religion. It is the one that says that if you wander away from this path, you are doomed. Doomed to hell, doomed to impossible karma, due to suffer for eternity. This was her invention she put in all teachings. This kept people in groups that were manageable and prevented them from wandering into truth. When this was revealed, she felt an immediate shift as we released it. She had also turned the world against me, or truth, or female energy. This is why I had such a reaction when she said she was a healer like me. She was not. I was working these lifetimes to undo the limitations that she had put on humanity. This is how the dynamics work in energy.

If you have a strong reaction to someone, trust it. If you can communicate with them, it may lead to an upgrade in awareness for all of humanity. Truth and love vibrate at similar frequencies. It is no wonder there is so little love in the world because there is so little truth. We are lied to and told to swallow the truth and be polite. But we are also thwarting love in the world as well. Truth is not mean spirited. It hurts because it is ripping off layers of illusion. But also, don't confuse truth for opinions. Most people are just steeped in opinions, so what they share would be mean because it is not truth.

This letter is not easy to write. It takes all my discipline and yet I am compelled to share. I hope it is received well.

-Freedom Health Success-

How Female Energy Differs from Male Energy

It is male energy that works so hard to have spiritual experiences and get out of the body. Female energy realizes that everything is already a spiritual experience and that we are not trapped in a body to begin with. Female energy just expands its consciousness to be anywhere and everywhere it desires, all at once.

-Joy Love Abundance-

Digging Deep to Release Imbalances

(Say each statement three times while tapping on your head and say it a fourth time while tapping on your chest.)

"We break down the walls of resistance between the balance of yin and yang; in all moments."

"We release the resistance of male energy to concede; in all moments."

"We release the resistance of female energy to empower herself; in all moments."

"We release the imbedded roots of the ego; in all moments."

"We release the contempt for transcendence; in all moments."

-Freedom Health Success-

Come Make Salt with Me

It takes me four hours to write the daily Letter of Accord that I send out. It is my first writing of the day and I send it out to anyone who requests it. I am tapped into truth and told what to write and am surprised each morning of what

I put in the letters. It is things that people have suspected in their hearts and it is a validation for them to see it in print.

After I write the letter, I get dizzy from the higher consciousness it taps into. I send it out and immediately get very sleepy. This is because I am dropping into the dream state to assist in the dispensing of truth as people read it.

This morning, as I dropped into the dream state, it felt like I was still awake in the physical world but things were a little different. This is being awake in the astral plane and in your astral body. So many of you are doing this now. The astral plane looks like the physical world with slight differences.

In the astral plane, the hawk that shows up in my backyard, was sitting in the upper room of my garage, perched in the front window looking out. He is a comfort to me and supports my writing and how I push the envelope in what I share.

In the dream, there was a woman who was being trapped in this man's house. It was a frat house and he seemed like a normal guy. But for some reason, I went to visit a woman who was staying in the house. When I got there, she was terrified. She was made to pose for a long time in one position like a doll. She was crying to herself underneath the stifled terror.

I looked around better and saw the apartment like a huge

dollhouse. On the left side of the house, all the rooms were depicted like you would see a doll house set up with open rooms. As I looked, I realized that there were a lot of women trapped in that dollhouse. They looked like literal Barbie dolls. They were trapped in that imagery and forced to stay in a fixed position to please the man who collected them. He was an insane brute.

He would invite the women into his home in a comely guise and then turn into the insane brute and hold them captive. I came in and turned them back into real women and held the insane man trapped at the end of the room as they all escaped. What I was doing was freeing female energy that has been held hostage for a timeless amount of time by male energy. I was literally freeing women from bondage. They were being terrorized at the hands of male energy.

In the dream there were also some quirky scenarios about making salt. There was a whole contraption set up to assist me in making salt. A man who helps me write my books and reach more people to assist kept bothering me in the dream with all these attempts of making salt. We were making it in the basement. We were getting it done. It was a very important symbolism.

When I awoke I felt that this dream was important. My Guides told me the symbolism in the dream. They told me that the Hawk totem was taking the truth of what I share and dispersing it to humanity while I sleep. In my past life as Helena Blavatsky, I wrote a book that was used as inspiration for Gandhi.

In his life, his huge act of defiance was making salt when it was illegal for Indians to do so. It was the turning point for the freedom of the Indian people as they claimed their own empowerment by making salt. When I woke, I was told that what I write is even more defiant that Gandhi making salt. Me sharing truth is having a sweeping effect of freeing humanity from the bonds of spiritual enslavement. My writings for humanity are parallel to Gandhi's practice of teaching the Indian people to make salt. They are freeing humanity from the shackles of spiritual slavery.

As I received this interpretation from my guides, the Hawk appeared in my apple tree and sat there present for me as an affirmation of this truth.

If you wish to continue to make salt with me, read my posts and share what I write with others. You can find me at www.jenward.com.

-Joy Love Abundance-

Androgyny As an Expression of Freedom

When a baby is born, what is the first label we are excited to put on it? Is it a boy or is it a girl? We base everything about the baby on that label: Clothes, colors, toys, interactions and activities. Why? Why is it so important? In past eras, it was important to know for the survival of the clan. Boys meant protection and strength, and girls meant propagation of the species.

We are long past those things mattering. The species has proven itself able to survive and no longer is brute strength necessary to protect the clan. So why is it so important? Some religious teachings mandate propagation. This is probably because, in more brutal eras, people may have most likely killed off their young for their own survival. They would need divine intervention to prevent the selfishness of man to kill out its own kind.

Being all male or a girly girl are the opposite ends of the gender polarity. These can be attractive to some, but there is also the sensitive guy or the tomboy who is very attractive and not such a polarized expression of a particular gender. There is so much personality and flavor in a person who isn't at one total end of the gender spectrum. We don't need people to be so polarized anymore. The race will survive. We no longer need to propagate the species. In fact, if we can pull out of that primal or habitual urge, the other species of the world and natural resources could have some breathing space, literally.

What is happening more and more is that people aren't at the extremes of the gender spectrum so much. More and more, people are discovering that it is difficult to define themselves as male or female. The fault with them is still thinking they need to. There is no need. They are the new norm. They are experiencing a new freedom.

To be androgynous is to be more comfortable with both experiences of male and female. But because society hasn't caught up to the reality of such an expression of freedom, they make the individual feel like they need to choose a gender. This is wrong. There is no need. To stay beautifully undefined is a form of empowerment.

Did you ever have someone ask a question and once they heard your answer they were less interested? The way for androgynous people to stay empowered is to not give an answer, especially when it isn't necessary. There is no reason for an androgynous person to define themselves for another. The real reason people want to know is they are interested in your sexual interactions or relationships. It is not their business.

How about this: stay androgynous. Stay undefined. Stay non-polarized. Stay non-linear. Refuse to choose. Refuse to define yourself. Refuse to give an answer to this question as if this answer reveals who you are in one word. How silly is that? Nobody needs to choose if they don't want to. We have all been both sexes many times over. There is little freedom or new expression in that. But to embrace all of your gender experiences and not limit yourself to one polarization is a new paradigm. It is a new freedom.

It is inevitable that society will become less polarized in its sexuality. This is natural, and it is does not need to show up as a perversion. People born with this freedom do not need to act out as a reaction to their beautiful self. To be androgynous is a very natural upgrade in the evolution of people. I hope this post makes its way to anyone struggling with gender identification. I hope it saves one person from mutilating their anatomy just to conform to an outmoded mentality.

It is a freeing and heroic experience to be fearlessly undefined. It is something to be proud of. To anyone who is experiencing feelings of androgyny, release the shame or the need to define yourself. Just be patient and wait for the rest of society to catch up. You are blessed and you are loved. Of course, do anything that makes you appreciate yourself more. But don't do it to conform to society. They are running to catch up to you.

-Freedom Health Success-

Addressing Male Domination

"These taps are done on behalf of humanity; in all moments."

"Enslavement to male energy is removed; in all moments."

"All shackles to male energy are removed; in all moments."

"All vivaxes with male energy are removed; in all moments."

"All tentacles to male energy are removed; in all moments."

"The claws of male energy are removed from our

Beingness; in all moments."

"All programming and conditioning from male energy is removed; in all moments."

"All engrams of male energy are removed; in all moments."

"All energy matrices of male energy are sent into the light and sound to dissolve; in all moments."

"All complex energy matrices of male energy are escorted into the light and sound by our guides to dissolve; in all moments."

"All energy is removed from male energy; in all moments."

"All glass ceilings of male energy are removed; in all moments."

"All illusion is stripped off of male energy; in all moments."

"All masks, walls, and armor are removed from male energy; in all moments."

"All the pain, burden, and limitations from male energy are removed; in all moments."

"All the controlling devises of male energy are removed; in all moments."

"All the fear, futility, and unworthiness caused by male energy is removed; in all moments."

"All the anger, self-righteousness, and arrogance of male energy is removed; in all moments."

"All the ignorance and illusion of separateness caused by male energy is removed; in all moments."

"All that male energy has taken is returned; in all moments."

"All that male energy has wounded is healed; in all moments."

"All that male energy has fragmented is made whole; in all moments."

"All imbalances of male energy are extracted from the universal sound frequency; in all moments."

"All imbalances of male energy are extracted from the universal light emanation; in all moments."

-Joy Love Abundance-

4: GAIA

CONNECT TO THE EARTH: A First Time Client's Dramatic Session

Recently, I facilitated a private remote session with a new client. Her good friend has been having sessions with me and she has seen the profound shift in her friend, so she was receptive to my work. This helps because of how deep the sessions work. The more of a trust factor that I have with the client, the more profound shift that can happen. When setting up the session, she said that she had no real issues except for dealing with an ex-partner whom she was going to be meeting with. Of course, I realized that that was not the case. It never is that simple.

As soon as we connected, I realized how receptive that she was. I perceived a deep loneliness in her. She also facilitated energy work in the form of massage therapy but when she was taught to allow the clients issues to flow into the earth to release through her feet, she was merely jamming it all into her body. She was not energetically following through. So she was jammed packed with a lot of issues of her own and all of her clients. At the beginning of the session, she felt like iron.

The reason this happened came through later in the session. It touched on a current theme that ran through her lifetimes. It was a profound insight for her to realize and it made certain sense to her when it was revealed. She had lost both her legs during a past life and so the ingrained memory or habit of that (what I call an engram), was preventing the energy from flowing down her legs and into the ground. There was a disconnect between he the earth and her.

"I release feeling disconnected from the earth; in all moments."

"I connect to the earth; in all moments."

"I recycle all energy back into love by perpetually pouring it into the earth; in all moments."

As I led her through instructions as to how to do the taps, she had a very difficult time doing them. The instructions are: Say each statement three times while tapping on your head and say it a fourth time while tapping on your chest. She said that she had a disability of some kind that prevented her from following simple instructions. I understand that because I experience a similar thing. So I challenged her, which brought another emotional round of tears.

I explained to her that she thinks beyond linear thought just like I do. So every time that she is giving instructions, she has to take time to translate it back into the tedious method of linear thought and it appears that she is slow. I reassured her that all of humanity is moving beyond linear thought and she is just ahead of the curve. Explaining that she is disabled is the only way to explain to those who only know linear thought about what is happening. I do that too. But I did not want her believing her own explanation when she really is so advanced. In fact, one of the first taps I led her through had to do with her first lifetime on earth and how lonely that was.

"I release feeling abandoned on earth; in all moments."

"I release rejecting earth; in all moments."

For many people, their first lifetime on earth is a sore disappointment. Living on earth compared to other planets is like being immersed in a sarcophagus. It is that stifling. Plus, on other planets we have had a beautiful long, powerful tail. So many people, when they get on earth, have trouble balancing with just the two legs instead of the powerful tripod that having legs and a tail affords. These people may have trouble with their lower back, tailbone or hips. She confirmed that she had chronic issues with her hip. She was surprised when she felt a release with the next tap.

"I release the trauma of losing my tail; in all moments."

"I reattach my tail; in all moments."

These taps, as strange as they were to her consciously, brought great relief to the whole hip area. She felt space in her hip area that was not there before, and we both felt heat in her lower back. I worked at moving stagnant energy through her whole spine and out. This released the issues that were jamming her up energetically.

"I remove all the anger that I have stored in my beingness;

in all moments."

"I release cursing earth; in all moments."

"I release hating earth; in all moments."

I have been told by my guides a while ago that people who defile the earth so easily have little affinity for it. They have been brought here begrudgingly, so they treat the earth as if they are disgruntled children who resent their home situations. They need to awaken to gratitude for being here on earth and release old grudges of being brought to this planet unwittingly. They need to stop looking up at the stars to be saved and accept that all their old friends from their home planet have already incarnated here. In an indirect way, this will assist in relieving the pillaging of earth that is happening through the rape of all its fossil fuels.

"I release waiting to be rescued from earth; in all moments."

"I release looking to the stars for redemption; in all moments."

"I accept my earthly conditions; in all moments."

"I release the systemic rape of earth; in all moments."

Many people who pray to the heavens were initially waiting to be saved from the fate of being on earth by their native planet. But now, it merely dissipates earth's energy. People need to accept that they are here on earth and pour their love and energy back into the earth or it will eventually be depleted as it is run to the ground and all its energy is dissipated.

"I release dissipating the earth of its energy; in all moments."

"I release diluting my energy by pouring into space; in all moments."

"I release diluting the earth's empowerment; in all moments."

The next issues that were revealed in my new client, who was amazed that she was having such profound shifts of energy so quickly, had to do with the experiences that were creating trauma during lifetimes on earth.

"I release being turned into a eunuch; in all moments."

"I release the trauma of having my legs cut off; in all moments."

Underneath that trauma, another past life revealed itself where she was lobotomized. That thing that she called a disability in herself, even though she was perfectly healthy, was a past life engram of the trauma of being lobotomized.

"I release the trauma of being lobotomized; in all moments."

As I led her through this tap, the energy in her head opened up and she felt light and expansive. I felt the issue in her right frontal lobe that was being addressed and repaired. She felt it too. She was not the same person that she was at the beginning of the session or who she had been for many lifetimes. She seemed to now be able to formulate the taps much more easily.

I asked her if she felt lighter and she did. I always describe this feeling as being like a Mylar balloon. She described it as being expansive like coral. This was an issue. Coral is not contained. This told me that the natural casing on her energy field was compromised. This casing is the Wei Chi. I led her through the taps to repair the Wei Chi, not only on her physical body, but also herself on the astral, causal and mental realms as well.

"I repair and fortify the Wei Chi of all my bodies; in all moments."

"I align all my bodies; in all moments."

"I am centered, empowered and immersed in divine love; in all moments."

After this, I addressed the theme that was running through her lifetimes. She was always having appendages cut off. It was creating a systemic cringing in her energy field. When I told her this and about the lobotomy, it was very validating to her. She suddenly realized why she felt flawed and incapacitated at the core. The taps and the understanding together worked to create a drastic shift in her. She also recalled how difficult it was for her to watch anyone get cut on a show. She was excited to note the reaction it caused in her and this validated what I was revealing about her.

Because it was a recurring theme, we addressed the first time that she ever got cut. This is called the initial cause or first cause. Since we work with all the lifetimes of a person at once, the way to remedy a reoccurring unwanted theme is to eliminate the first cause, or the first time it ever happened in all the lifetimes of that person. It is like the events are a line of dominoes and we remove that first domino that knocks down all the other dominoes.

"I eliminate the first cause in regards to being cut into; in all moments."

"I eliminate the first cause in regards to having appendages cut off; in all moments."

This was the new client's very first introduction to my work. She thought she was contacting me for a superficial reason. But she innately knew that what we would address would work so much more deeply. After working so deeply, I did address the more superficial issues that motivated her to desire a session with me. But her life is ever changed by this investment of an hour with me.

There was much more that we released. We released all the vows that she had taken in lifetimes of monastery living and issues with relationships. But the taps that I shared above are the ones that brought the deepest, most profound and drastic shifts to her energy. May you feel a shift as well by reading this and doing the taps.

Honoring Gaia

(Say each statement three times out loud while continuously tapping on the top of your head at the crown chakra; say it a fourth time while tapping on your heart chakra.)

"I release desecrating Gaia; in all moments."

"I release condoning the desecrating of Gaia; in all moments."

"I release the trauma of my fist life on earth; in all moments."

"I release treating the earth like a hostile world; in all moments."

"I release being stranded amongst the barbarians; in all moments."

"I release the trauma of being abandoned on a loveless world; in all moments."

"I release hating earth; in all moments."

"I release treating the earth like it's an evil stepmother; in all moments."

"I release desecrating the earth; in all moments."

"I release the devastating isolation of being left to inbreed amongst the barbarians; in all moments."

"I release mourning my home planet; in all moments."

"I release creating negative experiences to conjure up the vibration of my home planet; in all moments."

"I release morning my tail; in all moments."

"I release feeling helpless without my tail; in all moments."

"I release waiting to be rescued; in all moments."

"I shift my paradigm from resenting earth to respecting and appreciating Gaia; in all moments."

"I heal all resentment of the earth with my love and respect for Gaia; in all moments."

"I heal the earth with my purity and sanctity of my love; in all moments."

"I am centered and empowered in my love and respect for Gaia; in all moments."

"I hold a loving intention for the wellbeing of earth and all its loving inhabitants; in all moments."

-Freedom Health Success-

Who You Are

As a dynamic being you are not flawed. You are a whole complete loving sovereign energy watching the dynamics of you play out and trying to pour as much of that wisdom into the little human self as possible. That is the game. To see how much empowerment you can infuse into yourself. See? That is the shift. Shift into that dynamic omniscient expression of you and operate this physical life from that vantage point.

-Joy Love Abundance-

The Problem with Female Energy

The problem with female energy is that it isn't ego driven or goal oriented at all costs. It is happy to see everyone win and everyone do well. It will wait for others to catch up and it will assist everyone in feeling empowered. Everyone matters. If the world feels slow to catch up to where it should be, that is evidence that it is happening. When we feel that nothing is happening, the most is getting accomplished.

Take that rest you need from trying and pushing. It is no longer a competition of survival. We have entered the win/win mode and have adopted win/win modus operandi. Be kind to yourselves, be kind to others. There is no need to be the best anymore. There is simply maintaining the best qualities possible.

Accepting One's Own Nature

(Say each statement three times out loud while continuously tapping on the top of your head at the crown chakra and say it a fourth time while tapping on your heart chakra.)

"I release complaining about the weather; in all moments."

"I release being disgruntled with life; in all moments."

"I release wasting energy on complaints; in all moments."

"I release fighting my own nature; in all moments."

"I release undermining Gaia; in all moments."

"I release cursing Gaia, in all moments."

"I release complaining about Gaia; in all moments."

"I release desecrating Gaia; in all moments."

"I release negating my own nature; in all moments."

"I release the disconnect between myself and Gaia; in all moments."

"I release the belief that I am separate from Gaia; in all moments."

"I release having discord within myself; in all moments."

"I accept Gaia as my nature; in all moments."

"I shift my paradigm to be in agreement with nature; in all moments."

"I am centered and empowered in my love and appreciation for Gaia; in all moments."

"I resonate and emanate love and appreciation for Gaia; in all moments."

-Joy Love Abundance-

The Miracle of You

Kindness is my prayer

Encouragement is my song

Sincerity is my anthem

Singing it makes me strong

Connectedness is my motto

Service is my decree

Helping others is my virtue

Doing so sets me free

Taking is sometimes giving

Receiving graciously is a gift

Justice is spontaneous

The law of Love works swift

Everything you think

Everything you do

Is meant to excel you further

Into the miracle of you

If denial is your option

Ignorance is it too

Intelligence isn't awareness

That's what smart people misconstrue

Awareness leads from the heart

Intelligence may follow

A good mind without the heart

Can leave one cold and hollow

But a heart with pure intention

Has warmth and depth to spare

That is how they're recognized

They have ample love to share.

-Freedom Health Success-

Put an End to This Selfish Act

I admonished another dear soul for their selfish shortcoming. It is the only flaw that is not acceptable. They refused a gesture of kindness from me. They do not realize how thoughtless an act that is. The whole universe exists as fluid energy passing through all souls. The way to bring this beautiful synchronicity to a grinding halt is to refuse to receive. It is far more acceptable to refuse to give than to refuse to receive. It is far more damaging to refuse to receive.

When someone with a fluid energy gives, there is a force behind that. When it hits a wall, it is energetically damaging. It is similar to a fast moving car hitting a brick wall. That is what happens when one refuses to receive. The world is paralyzed in such actions. There are those of us working to untangle deep-rooted knots by perpetual giving. The only the kind thing to do is to allow this force to move unencumbered through the world by accepting the gifts that are presents.

Refusing to receive, on an energetic level, has been a tactical means of paralyzing energy and stopping the flow of love in the world. Please don't be a part of it. Please accept gifts when you can and do your part. The gifts perpetually abound. So please start receiving.

Prophetic Dreams of a Wise One

A dear friend who has the most dynamic dreams shared two different dreams with me. They explain the dynamics that are going on between male and female energy in the world.

The first one she told me about had an alpha male acquaintance in it. He kept begging her to come back to him. This was odd because they were never in a relationship. He kept begging and begging, but she stood her ground. He finally relinquished, and in doing so, took off a ring and gave it to her. It felt like she was being freed of him and getting her power back.

In the second dream, there was a businessman that has benefited from doing the taps. In the dream he was so happy and enthusiastic. He is a very nice man but in the dream he was trying to fit my friend for shoes. He insisted that she wear business attire black loafers. She told him that she didn't need the shoes but he didn't hear her.

These dreams are conveying how the paradigm shift in the world is being processed by individuals. On some level, male energy knows that woman is being empowered. So he is trying to win her back. He is almost insistent on it. This may be reflecting in your lives. The man grants the woman her freedom even though it isn't his to grant.

Then, male energy starts getting on board with female energy being empowered. So he wants to help. He believes it is going to look like male energy. That is why the man was insisting on the woman wearing business shoes. He insists that female energy show up similar to male energy. This is not necessarily the case.

Things are changing. Lies are being uncovered, elephants are retiring, women are being empowered, people are dropping their facades and individuals are standing their ground. They are showing up original and unique; and blurring the lines.

-Freedom Health Success-

Have Goodness Prevail

My Easter gift to the world is assisting female energy to prevail and for the world to attain a balance.

(Say each statement three times while tapping on your head and say it a fourth time while tapping on your chest.)

"All negative portals are collapsed and dissolved; in all moments."

"All negative energy in the world is dissipated; in all moments."

"I think, speak, observe, and love in energy; in all moments."

"The world thinks, speaks, observes, and loves in energy;

in all moments."

"All imbalances in the world are dissipated; in all moments."

"All self-righteous taking in the world is alleviated; in all moments."

"All portals of self-righteous taking are collapsed and dissolved; in all moments."

"All portals of apathy and ignorance are collapsed and dissolved; in all moments."

"All engrams of repetitious behavior are washed away; in all moments."

"All engrams of programming and conditioning are washed away; in all moments."

"All engrams of enslavement are washed away; in all moments."

"All engrams of imprisonment are washed away; in all moments."

"All portals to female defilement are collapsed and dissolved; in all moments."

"All engrams to female defilement are washed away; in all moments."

"All portals to male domination are collapsed and dissolved; in all moments."

"All engrams of male domination are washed away; in all moments."

"Space is made in the world for goodness to prevail; in all moments."

"All blockages to goodness prevailing in the world are removed; in all moments."

"Propensity for goodness to prevail in the world is expanded; in all moments."

"The world is centered and empowered in goodness prevailing; in all moments."

"The world resonates, emanates, and is interconnected with all life in goodness prevailing; in all moments."

-Freedom Health Success-

Honor Gaia

"I am a conscious Gaia energetic; in all moments."

"I dissolve all firewalls of obscuration; in all moments."

"I remove all blinders from humanity; in all moments."

"I lay down the ego for the betterment of humanity; in all moments."

"I assist humanity in laying down the ego for the betterment of Humanity; in all moments."

"I hear the inner notes of freedom; in all moments."

"I sing the inner notes of freedom; in all moments."

"I exponentially amplify the light; in all moments."

"I exponentially amplify the sound; in all moments."

"I make space in this world for Gaia communities to be realized; in all moments."

"I remove all blockages to Gaia communities be realized; in all moments."

"I revise all prior pathways to Gaia communities; in all moments."

"I stretch humanity's capacity to revise all prior pathways to Gaia; in all moments."

"I shift my paradigm from humanity to Humanity; in all moments."

"I shift humanity's paradigm to Humanity's paradigm; in all moments."

"I am centered and empowered in the flowering of Humanity; in all moments."

-Joy Love Abundance-

Full Moon Celebration

These powerful taps were given today to assist everyone in embracing their higher self. They also help in assisting humanity and any trapped souls that are not so free to embrace their empowerment. Today is a great portal to assist in a shift for all of life. Please celebrate with all the wonders of the Universe by doing this exercise.

(Say each statement three times out loud while CONTINUOUSLY tapping on the top of your head at the crown chakra and say it a fourth time while tapping on your chest at the heart chakra. Say each word deliberately. They are not just words but a vibration that you are initiating to shift energy. Pause after each word. Say it in a commanding but even tone, not as a question. Forgo saying it in a singsong tone or with bravado. Say them all.)

"I declare myself a surrogate for all life in doing these taps, in all moments."

"I heal all emotional scars, in all moments."

"I heal all causal wounds, in all moments."

"I remove all programming and conditioning, in all moments."

"I remove all engrams, in all moments."

"I send all energy matrices into the light that separate me from Divine Love, in all moments."

"I release compartmentalizing my universe, in all moments."

"I release demonizing the heart of another; in all moments."

"I send all energy matrices into the light that give me the need to defend my status; in all moments."

"I send all energy matrices into the light that trap my essence; in all moments."

"I send all energy matrices into the light that compartmentalize my beingness; in all moments."

"I send all energy matrices into the light that motivate me with fear; in all moments."

"I release the fear of my own greatness; in all moments."

"I release confusing my greatness with overwhelming responsibility; in all moments."

"I release denying the possibility of my greatness realized; in all moments."

"I release visiting the third dimensional me on the fifth dimensional me; in all moments."

"I remove all vivaxes between the fifth dimensional me and the third dimensional me; in all moments."

"I remove all tentacles between the fifth dimensional me and the third dimensional me; in all moments."

"I remove all programming and conditioning that the third dimensional me has put on me; in all moments."

"I remove all engrams that the third dimensional me has put on me; in all moments."

"I send all energy matrices into the light that visit the third dimensional me on the fifth dimensional me; in all moments."

"I recant all vows and agreements between myself and the third dimensional me; in all moments."

"I release the fear of losing my essence in releasing the third dimensional me; in all moments."

"I remove all curses between myself and the third dimensional me; in all moments."

"I remove all blessings between myself and the third dimensional me; in all moments."

"I sever all strings and cords between myself and the third dimensional me; in all moments."

"I dissolve all karmic ties between myself and the third dimensional me; in all moments."

"I remove all the pain, burden, limitations, and illusion of separateness that the third dimensional me has put on me; in all moments."

"I take back all that third dimensional me has taken from me; in all moments."

"I withdraw all my energy from the third dimensional me; in all moments."

"I release resonating with the third dimensional me; in all moments."

"I release the fifth dimensional me resonating with the third dimensional me; in all moments."

"I release the fifth dimensional me emanating with the third dimensional me; in all moments."

"I extract all third dimensional me from the fifth dimensional me's sound frequency; in all moments."

"I extract all the third dimensional me from the fifth dimensional me's light emanation; in all moments."

"I shift my paradigm from the third dimensional me to the fifth dimensional me; in all moments."

"I transcend the third dimensional me; in all moments."

"I am centered and empowered in the fifth dimensional me and above; in all moments."

-Freedom Health Success-

Female Energy Redistributing Energy

I have been doing very active energy work to starve out power and greed in the world. I know it sounds naive to some, but those who know me, know what I do. I am not done in returning all that has been depleted from the earth. But now it is in a better position to nurture and replenish itself again. It is our responsibility to nurture it in return with gratitude and kindness to all. Just saying.

-Joy Love Abundance-

Bursting Bubbles of Illusion

I am confident now of my spiritual prowess and yet know that I am flawed. If dynamic spirituality meant perfection, then I would be perfect. I am not. I am proud now to help debunk the myth that being spiritually dynamic means physical perfection.

Everyone can now relax in the myriad of beautiful chaotic dichotomies that they are. Being rigid in a hell bent single pointed view of perfection is missing the mark. We dance, cry, sing, wallow and immerse ourselves in blurring the lines of all mental concepts. That is our sprite-like quality poking a stick at conformity. We are bursting each bubble of illusion as joyfully as popping soap bubbles against the backdrop of a sun-filled day.

A Message from Earth Herself

A dear friend came over the day before my birthday. She had a bad dream about something negative manipulating a family member. She was very upset. I am using my birthday as a day to give all I can out to others, so I was going to use the day before my birthday to rest and enjoy a free flowing day. But she was upset, so I told her to come right over and I would assist her.

We did a couple hours of energy work on the topic of power disguised as female energy and controlling the youth of humanity. It was amazing work that caused a lot of shifts within us as we did them. We sat outside under the apple tree and I instructed her in doing the taps. She kept interrupting me and losing my place as much as she tried to do them right.

My whole dynamic of my day shifted to do this work with her. It was really necessary but she kept sabotaging the taps that I gave her by saying them wrong or saying them before me and losing my place. Suddenly I got really angry with her. It was no longer me.

I was energetically very pointed with her. I asked her why she is so guarded about what I do when she benefits the most. Why does she not share openly about how I help her when she is the one who witnesses it daily? Why does she not advocate for me and my goodness? Why does she allow her friends and family to ignore and dismiss me? I was very hard on her.

I said that she must be using me. She loves benefitting from the taps and my help and feeling empowered. But she still does not share all that she has experienced. I explained to her that while she is feeling good and empowered about herself, there are others around the world suffering badly. How can she be so complacent when so many around the world are crying out for help and I have the means to assist? I kept asking her questions. Why is she ashamed of goodness? Why does she protect others from knowing goodness?

I said to her, "You are not talking to Jen right now. This is earth." My friend said later that my demeanor and whole look changed right then. Earth continued. "I am so tired. Why do you not help me? Why do you not encourage people to help me? When you ignore Jen, you ignore me. When you dismiss what she does, you are working against me. Don't I give everything to you? Why do you not want to help me?"

"You think it is about Jen being known in the world. She doesn't care about that. That is work to her. Jen wants to be validated because she wants me to be validated. She is doing everything she can to help me. Why won't you help her? Why won't you make it easier for her? Why don't you make it easier for me? Do you think it matters to Jen whether people know her? She is advocating for me.

"But you who sit here and benefit most from her love and kindness, still deny her. You deny me. Don't I give you air and beauty? Do I ever deny you? Has Jen ever denied you? Why won't you help me? If it were just about her, everything she does would go unheard and she would just die in a broken body, but that is okay. It has happened again and again. But I need your help and you can help by pouring love into me. Pour love into Jen."

At one point my friend glazed over. Earth called her on it. It got suddenly cold and overcast. "You have decided to check out," Earth said. "That is fine. Do what you will. You will still have a nice life. No worries but don't lie to us or to yourself. Just go!"

My friend got upset and cried instantly that she wanted to help. It was strange just how quickly, the sun and warmth returned after she said that. I told her to ask the tree about what I was saying. She grabbed the tree behind her and said, "He says you are speaking truth."

Afterwards I cried in fits of sobbing as I held the tree for comfort. My body felt crippled and old and wanted to give out. I realized that this is not my body but how the earth is feeling. The difficulty in maintaining my balance is parallel to earth maintaining its orbit. Earth is tired. Earth is hurting. Earth is begging for help. Why am I one of the only few who hear it? Please help. She is begging for help yet too despondent from being denied to expect anything from anyone. That is how I feel. Do you see? That is exactly how I feel.

-Joy Love Abundance-

5: HEALING

You Deserve Wellness

When people have issues, many times they think in the worst-case scenario. Even when people are deciding whether they are coming down with the flu or something, they have to ruminate over the signs before they validate themselves by telling others they are sick.

Then they feel the need to defend those issues. They don't want to sound ridiculous so they build up a case for being sick. They are in a sense coming to agreement with the illness. Then they identify with it in a sense by defending their need to nurture themselves by having it.

Being sick is a chance to opt out for a bit. It is an excuse to stay home, relinquish the diet, forgo the work load, spoil yourself, relax, take a break, focus on yourself, feel important, be the center of attention, ask for help, surrender to life, allow others to help and change priorities. Because people are used to invalidating themselves otherwise, being sick is their chance to get fulfillment.

But then the novelty rubs off and the patients feel they have to return to “the grind” or up the anti on their illness. It is sad to think how many people up the anti. It is one of the main reasons dis-ease is so prevalent in society.

Here is a better way: take a day off, go off the diet once in awhile, spoil yourself, leave work at the office, be the center of attention, accept help, ask for help, change priorities, have fun, return to joy, return to ease. Create it! Demand it! Revel in it. What the human can endure is limited but what the human spirit can tap into is infinite.

Here are also some taps to help:

"I release validating myself through illness; in all moments."

"I release using illness to relate to others; in all moments." (this may happen in genetic diseases)

"I release my genetic propensity for disease; in all moments."

"I release carrying illness in my DNA; in all moments."

"I release using illness to feel special; in all moments."

"I release using illness as a common ground; in all moments."

"I release being in agreement with illness; in all moments."

"I remove being cursed with illness; in all moments."

"I dissolve all karmic ties with illness; in all moments."

"I remove all the pain, burden and limitations that illness has put on me; in all moments."

"I take back all the joy, love, abundance and freedom that illness has taken from me; in all moments."

"I release resonating with illness; in all moments."

"I release all illness from my sound frequency; in all moments."

"I release all illness from my light emanation; in all moments."

"I shift my paradigm from illness to joy, love, abundance and freedom; in all moments."

Let's return to Joy, Love, Abundance and Freedom. Those are birthrights worth striving for and what every loving parent wishes for their baby. You deserve a wonderful existence.

-Freedom Health Success-

Be a Light and Sound Activist

Anytime you say anything is hard, complain about something, own a condition by calling it "my" or describe yourself in negative terms, you are plastering the condition into the very fiber of your essence so that the condition is permanent. Think of yourself as an emanation of pure light and a frequency of pristine music woven together into form.

Here is a technique to loosen all the gunk that you have melded to you. Remember action follows thought. So all the negative thoughts you have collected on yourself unintentionally can be now be addressed with this conscious intention.

See yourself at the core as a beautiful, cosmic, egg shaped orb of pulsing fabric of energy. See it bright and glistening within, with a silvery bluish hue from the intensity of its emanation. But on the outer "skin" of it, see layers and layers of thoughts glued on with feelings that have covered its surface like ugly barnacles and chipped paint. It is repulsive to see such pristine beauty constricted in this way.

In your heart's eye, visualize, applying warm and soothing love to the whole orb of you, to loosen the paint and barnacles. See it like steaming a wallpaper to pull it off more easily. Now, imagine all the contaminants bubbling to the very outer surface to be removed. Visualize taking a paint scraper of some kind and scraping off all the old thoughts, opinions, beliefs, fears and experiences that have limited you from totally expressing your most dynamic self and owning your empowerment.

Feel the freedom of releasing all of these old stuck-on issues. They are the engrams that have imprinted on you to squelch the beauty of your sheen and your confidence. It is releasing all the defenses that caused you to play it safe. It may give you a sensation of being difficult to do like the pain of pulling one hair from your body. But that is evidence that you are being effective.

In life, this process would take a very long time, eons perhaps. Think of it as taking as long as it would take for the elements to wear away layers of old pain. In fact, realize that the things that bring you pain and difficulty in this life are like the wind eroding the layers that have constricted you from expressing your fullest essence as soul.

The beauty of this technique is that you can control the release of such issues, which is empowering to so many who are trying to express themselves fully. Because seemingly losing control over their situation in life is one of the main reasons they cling so dearly to the barnacles. For some twisted reason, holding on to them represents feeling empowered. This is the ruse. All of this tangled confusion is conveniently released through the practice of this exercise.

After one gets an understanding of when they are allowing barnacles to collect on their beautiful essence, it will be difficult not to address them right away. They will start to refrain from complaining, owning disease and saying things are hard because they don't want to feel those barnacles recollect on themselves. It may feel subtle but one may be aware of them almost like they would at having a sticker stuck on their hand or face.

As a gained benefit, people will start to understand what they are doing to others with their verbiage and their thoughts. So they will be more conscious of not putting limiting barnacles on others. There is a rawness and initial discomfort when these things are either scraped off or wear off gradually with pain. So people will see the benefit of not allowing them to attach in the first place. This is the wisdom behind Native Americans using sign language when they did have words to communicate. They were avoiding limiting themselves and others as much as possible.

By practicing this technique, people will start to realize that deeming issues or situations as sad is a way of singeing them into the energy field of the subject even if it is the whole world. People will understand when they are actually assisting in freeing humanity from a social issue, and when they are merely adding crust to the surface with their misguided intention of raising awareness.

Raising awareness was taught to us as a lie to enslave humanity more to whatever the issue was. In past generations, people would not even say the word cancer. Now all that raising awareness has done is made it something that everyone in society is now very familiar with. How does this free us? It does not.

After one has learned how to use this technique for their own benefit, they can also visualize scraping off all the barnacles from earth itself by envisioning it the same way. Issues like war, slavery, apathy, fear, power, and control are huge barnacles covering the energetic surface of earth. Loosen the issues by steaming the world with divine love. Then practice scraping all the paint and barnacles off. Perhaps there is a huge one covering one country. Perhaps it is what makes them more conducive to revenge, them versus us mode, mistrust or ruthless measures. These barnacles may have been plastered on the surface of their demographic years ago when perhaps they were the victims of a situation that they now believe themselves to be.

Perhaps people with loving hearts and pure intentions can do more to advance us towards world peace than all the activism that has existed through history. Please don't forget to remove the barnacles of arrogance, ignorance, monetary worship, entitlement and male domination. Feel the empowerment and the connection of other true Light and Sound activists in doing this work. Please feel my support and appreciation as well.

-Joy Love Abundance-

Release Being Broken In

Recently, I facilitated a private remote session with a dynamic healer. It was her first session so we were talking for the first time. Most people are very nervous when they call but she was not. She was engaging and quite aware. She immediately began to navigate the dynamics of the interaction. To assist her, I could not allow this.

I cut through the conversation with curtness. As she was being engaging and charming, I met her with, "I don't care." I told her it was not relevant to helping her. She was still engaging. But as she was engaging, I saw an image from her past playing out simultaneously that colored everything that she did. It was she as a young woman being pulled backwards into a dark room by her long braid to be raped and beaten into submission.

People cope in so many different ways. Her way of coping was to be so accomplished and so on top of everything. She was able to handle everything that came at her. She was using being dynamic as her form of denial. I had to take that crutch away from her so we could address the issue. In fact, she was so good at using her crutch that I saw all the interactions she had had with facilitators who could possibly have helped her with this issue. I saw her navigate them away from the issue by being so engaging.

When I was curt, she overlooked it as long as she could, but I would not relent. As lovely as she was, I was stark and indifferent to it. She finally responded with shutting down. The contrast was drastic. She did not know how to take me. She was no longer engaging, rather annoyed and probably sorry that she was working with me. I asked her if she hated authority figures. She confirmed that she did.

Then I explained the scenario that was playing out within her energy field over and over again of her being raped and beaten into submission. It resonated as her truth. We broke through the layers of defenses to the place that we needed to be so she could release this trauma. There were many screams and horrific cries to release the energy of the past experience as she performed the taps I gave her. It was a huge shift for her in one short hour.

Here are some of the taps that I led her through:

(Say each statement three times out loud while continuously tapping on the top of your head at the crown chakra and say it a fourth time while tapping on your heart chakra. Pause before “in all moments.”)

"I release the shame and trauma of being broken in; in all moments.”

"I release discontinuing to exist as a result of being broken in; in all moments.”

"I release confusing vulnerability with the trauma of being broken in; in all moments.”

"I release confusing vulnerability as losing a fight to exist; in all moments.”

"I release confusing the interplay with others as the struggle of being broken in; in all moments.”

"I release using competency to cope with the engrams of being broken in; in all moments.”

"I release being strangled by the memories of being broken in; in all moments.”

"I release being enslaved to the struggle of being broken in; in all moments.”

"I recant all vows and agreements between myself and being broken in; in all moments.”

"I remove all curses between myself and being broken in; in all moments."

"I sever all cords and ties between myself and being broken in; in all moments."

"I dissolve all karmic ties between myself and being broken in; in all moments."

"I remove all the pain, burden, limitations and engrams between myself and being broken in; in all moments."

"I take back all the joy, love, abundance, freedom, health, success, security, companionship, peace, life, wholeness, beauty, enthusiasm, wholeness, spirituality, enlightenment and confidence that being broken in has taken from me; in all moments."

"I withdraw all my energy from being broken in; in all moments."

"I repair and fortify the wei chi of all my bodies; in all moments."

"I release resonating with being broken in; in all moments."

"I release emanating with being broken in; in all moments."

"I extract all of being broken in from my sound frequency; in all moments."

"I extract all of being broken in from my light body; in all

moments."

"I shift my paradigm from being broken in to joy, love, abundance, freedom, health, success, security, companionship, peace, life, wholeness, beauty, enthusiasm, wholeness, spirituality, enlightenment and confidence; in all moments."

"I transcend being broken in; in all moments."

"I am centered and empowered in joy, love, abundance, freedom, health, success, security, companionship, peace, life, wholeness, beauty, enthusiasm, wholeness, spirituality, enlightenment and confidence; in all moments."

"I align all my bodies; in all moments."

"I am centered and empowered in divine love; in all moments."

It was unclear if she physically died or her spirit died from the experience in that lifetime. Regardless, the freedom of her being without this scenario playing out in her energy field constantly was profound. She was exhausted after the session because of the huge shift in energy within her. It is not the same as running a marathon, but it is a huge effort to shift so drastically. She got herself to sleep very early that night.

Overcoming Rape

It takes a lot of resilience to overcome being raped. For some people, it affects the rest of their life. Not only is it the trauma, but there are also feelings of self-doubt, worthiness, lingering fear and mourning the loss of innocence.

In a recent session, I felt it necessary to point out to my client that more people experience a traumatic sexual experience than experience a fairytale moment that we see in movies. With many, it is between those two ranges but important to point out. People who have been raped may think that they were robbed of something that everyone else has experienced and that may not necessarily be the case.

Here are some taps to help those suffering with the aftereffects of rape. There are so many listed because many people are suffering in silence. My suggestion is that you take the time to do these taps to empower yourself. You are not alone and you are very lovable. And if you know of someone who may benefit from these, please share.

"I release the trauma of being raped; in all moments."

"I release blaming myself for being raped; in all moments."

"I release the guilt and shame of being raped; in all moments."

"I release the fear of being raped; in all moments."

"I release the belief that I deserved to be raped; in all moments."

"I release the belief I caused the rape; in all moments."

"I release quantifying rape; in all moments."

"I release confusing rape for intimacy; in all moments."

"I release allowing intimacy to be shrouded by the rape; in all moments."

"I release being defined by the rape; in all moments."

"I release mourning my innocence; in all moments."

"I release the belief that I am sullied; in all moments."

"I release the fear of intimacy; in all moments."

"I release the belief that I am unlovable; in all moments."

"I release the belief that I am unworthy of love; in all moments."

"I erase the rape from my energy field; in all moments."

"I remove the rape cookies from my hard drive; in all moments."

"I reboot my system to Love; in all moments."

"I install intimacy software into my system; in all moments."

"I make space in this world for a loving, intimate relationship; in all moments."

"I remove all blockages to having a loving, intimate relationship; in all moments."

"I release sabotaging my love life; in all life times"

"I stretch my capacity to have a loving, intimate relationship; in all moments."

"I am centered in joy, love abundance, freedom and intimacy; in all moments."

-Joy Love Abundance-

The Subliminal Message of the Pink Campaign

In this particular neighborhood, all the garbage containers are pink. It is a gimmick to support the pink ribbon campaign. These campaigns tap into the passion of the individuals in their most personal plights and use that passion to promote a business.

And since so many of them are devoid of any real passion, they have to tap into the passion of the consumers and exploit it for their own gain. This is what the pink ribbon campaign is all about. If it didn't make money for a business, it would not happen. This is just one small way people are being exploited all over the world every day and in every way.

So the beautiful color that was assigned to depict the birth of our innocent little girls is now also allotted a treacherous disease. This is diminishing the value of little girls everywhere by subliminal association. But this one business took it further. Now, in this one neighborhood, innocent newborn girls are now subliminally associated with garbage. GARBAGE. This campaign is the antithesis of the empowerment of women. When people start to connect the dots, they will realize they have been duped in this matter for way too long.

Women who advocate for women may want to reject partaking in the subliminal program that is taking place in regards to women.

-Freedom Health Success-

The Healing Portal

What I do as a Healer is open up a portal for another reality for my clients to walk through. No wonder it was considered magic for so long. Only now, we have the scientific studies due to quantum and metaphysical studies to support it. I claim what I do and validate it in others who serve in this way. And if this sounds too out there, it is the exact same thing that a smile does.

-Joy Love Abundance-

The Scoop on Disease

We have all had trauma in our past lives. It is a fact. When we incarnate again, the memory of such things are stored in a hologram of our physical body and some of it bleeds through to this physical body. We all store it in different parts of our body depending upon the nature of the past trauma.

Say all those who died in the Crusades stored their pain in their upper shoulders and arms. All those who were hung, or decapitated hold pain in their neck. All those who have been enslaved may register it in their back. All those who have been murdered running for their life register it in their glandular system. All those who were tortured to death may carry it in their nervous system. Those who have been repeatedly raped and manhandled register pain to the touch as a means to keep others from touching them. All of these traumas and issues are coordinated in our DNA.

But the traumas are so horrific that we don't want to acknowledge them. To do even that brings excruciating fear and trauma to the conscious mind. So we go to the doctor and it is his job to give a label to each set of pain. This label is very important. This label is the proxy for our emotional issues without having to acknowledge the emotional issues. So instead of facing the fact that you were raped and passed around in a past life, the doctor gives you a diagnosis of ovarian cysts or cancer. That way, you can get sympathy and support for having the cysts without ever having to acknowledge the trauma. It's a win-win for those who want to stay in denial.

But if one wants to really be empowered and get past all their issues, they will forgo the luxury of the validation of a diagnosis and will use every method available to release the original trauma. That is what I do. I release the stagnant energy of the original cause. Giving one a diagnosis is a means to form a scab on the issue without ever cleansing the puss and ooze underneath. That is how it becomes systemic to the body and can create a life altering pathology that destroys the tissue and leaves the physical doctors to cut out body parts which brings secondhand trauma to an already taxed body.

This is insanity. Using disease as a proxy to stay in denial of underlying issues is a commonly used practice. But that doesn't mean that it isn't barbaric. It is one step up from using leeches to drain the body of negative spirits. In a way, at least that process was acknowledging problematic energy. We can all do better in our own empowerment. I am here to assist.

-Freedom Health Success-

The Physiological Exchange of Emotional Energy

It's common sense that if we drink a lot of water, we will have to relieve our bladder at some point of that water. But when it comes to ingesting anger, sadness, and other "heavy" emotions, we think that they are just magically transformed. Because we can't see them, we disconnect from the process of relieving them. Yet our verbiage tells us otherwise.

"Someone dumped on me today."

"I just had to talk it out."

"I have to bounce it off someone."

"I am taking in everything that you are saying."

We know that there is a need to get rid of these issues. The lazy way is to dump them onto some agreeable soul. This is pure ignorance to continue to do so. People are hurting their friends because they are too lazy to take action to convert the stagnant energy into a more productive form. Of course, some people are in a chronic state and they may need help of a professional who is equipped to deal with their barrage of emotional energy. But the rest of us should not have to be made to feel guilty by not being dumping grounds for a friend's issues. And that should not be the requirement of a friend or a commonality in friendship.

There are so many people who say they love their friends but have to limit their time with them because all the friend does is want to talk about their problems. The person will even get angry at the friend who tries to pull back and ask why they cut them off. They are cutting the friend off out of self-preservation. It is a necessary survival tool sometimes.

There are more self-responsible ways to convert this energy from stagnant emotional energy to something productive.

Journal: It is a safe and effective way of getting emotions out.

Exercise: It converts emotional energy into kinetic energy.

Self Improvement: It is converting negative energy into positive energy.

Help others: The feel good component will override that the resistance that the stored issues will invoke.

(That is all resistance is: stagnant emotional issues that

want to stay put.)

Just realizing that there is an exchange of energy in every interaction will make people more conscious and responsible as to what they bring to the table. For example, the reason why people get irritable when they are dieting is because all the anger that they stored in the liver is now being separated from the fat they stored and is now manifesting in the state it came to the individual in. How many overweight people have people or situations in their life that are overwhelming? Being overweight isn't about being greedy for food; it is about needing a base substance of fat in which to store the emotional issues that are being carried. People are literally eating problems.

People need to be trained how to treat each other. When some people secure a session with me, they think they will be dumping all their angst onto me. I cannot allow that. When I try to explain that I cannot process all the emotions that they want to pass over, that I merely unhook them from them and send them away, they feel frustrated and may continue to energetically vomit on me. I consider it rude at some point, and if they continue, I may choose not to interact with them in the future. It is not honoring an agreement to dump on others. My way is effective. Their way may serve themselves, but it doesn't serve their target victim, aka friend.

Some people look for horrific things to put on their status page. They know they are affecting others. It makes them feel important. People know that it feels good to unload on their page because good people are reading it and taking it in for them. They are disconnected by the affect of their actions and just are indulging in the "feel good" component of it.

If you are someone that people find to dump on, you may want to look at that. It may feel good short term to listen to someone and make them feel good, but how does it serve you in the long run? Is your life running smoothly? How is your health? I guarantee that many of the people who have fibromyalgia are the caring, nurturing types. I have told a few of them to purge from nurturing others for a while. But they have been incapable of doing that because that is how their sense of self is being fed.

If you are being dumped on, share this page. The next time someone starts to dump, stop them and shift to something neutral. Explain that it doesn't feel good to your wellbeing to listen to their problems. If they understand, then they care about you. If they react, they are inadvertently using you for their own wellbeing. If they continue, tell them to please stop and continue to advocate for yourself by even telling them to shut up if you have to. Make the distinction between caring about them but not caring about hearing their issues. If they still continue, you may have to cut them off.

Your wellbeing and your sense of wholeness is your first priority. It is your first job in life to maintain your own balance. Your happiness and sense of balance are never on the table as a bargaining chip for friendship. But a friend's respect of your boundaries and a sense of responsibility in interacting with you are on the table. You hold all the cards. Play your hand wisely!

Stay Balanced

Say each statement three times out loud while continuously tapping on the top of your head at the crown chakra, and say it a fourth time while tapping on your chest.

"I release vacillating between unworthiness and pride; in all moments."

"I release vacillating between poverty and abundance; in all moments."

"I release vacillating between fear and love; in all moments."

"I release vacillating between confidence and insecurity; in all moments."

"I release vacillating between joy and sorrow; in all moments."

"I release vacillating between acceptance and rejection; in all moments."

"I release vacillating between sickness and health; in all moments."

"I release vacillating between love and hate; in all moments."

"I release vacillating between slavery and freedom; in all moments."

"I release vacillating between conflict and peace; in all moments."

"I release vacillating between failure and success; in all moments."

"I release vacillating between companionship and isolation; in all moments."

"I release vacillating between creativity and conformity; in all moments."

"I release vacillating between death and life; in all moments."

"I release vacillating between complaints and gratitude; in all moments."

"I release vacillating between darkness and light; in all moments."

"I release vacillating between beauty and ugliness; in all moments."

"I release vacillating between ignorance and enlightenment; in all moments."

"I release vacillating between criticism and gratitude; in all moments."

"I release vacillating between poverty and abundance; in all

moments."

"I release vacillating between enthusiasm and apathy; in all moments."

"I release vacillating between fragmentation and wholeness; in all moments."

"I release vacillating between poverty and abundance; in all moments."

"I release vacillating between fear and love; in all moments."

"I hold a steady and even stance within joy, love, abundance, freedom, health, success, peace, life, wholeness, beauty, enthusiasm confidence, light and enlightenment; in all moments."

"I am centered and empowered in joy, love, abundance, freedom, health, success, peace, life, wholeness, beauty, enthusiasm confidence, light and enlightenment; in all moments."

Return the Sacredness of Water to the World

"I declare myself a surrogate for the world in doing these taps; in all moments."

"All water pollution is eliminated; in all moments."

"All desecration of sacred water is eliminated; in all moments."

"All enslavement to polluting sacred water is released; in all moments."

"All illusion is stripped off of water polluters; in all moments."

"All vivaxes with water pollution are removed; in all moments."

"All karmic imbalances with sacred water are eliminated; in all moments."

"All desperation due to water pollution is eradicated; in all moments."

"All apathy and indifference towards water pollution is removed; in all moments."

"All urge to disengage from caring about our sacred water is removed; in all moments."

"The poisoning of our sacred water is eliminated; in all moments."

"All masks, walls, and armor on all those who pollute our sacred water are removed; in all moments."

"All minimizing of the importance of our sacred water is removed; in all moments."

"All psychic attacks by those who cause water pollution are dissipated; in all moments."

"Desecration of sacred water is untangled from mass consciousness; in all moments."

"Desecration of sacred water is stripped away from mass consciousness; in all moments."

"All poisoning due to the desecration of sacred water is eliminated; in all moments."

"All tentacles with those that poison sacred water are severed; in all moments."

"All programming and conditioning due to water pollution are removed; in all moments."

"All engrams of desecration of sacred water are removed; in all moments."

"All energy and support for those who cause water pollution are withdrawn; in all moments."

"All muscle memory of water pollution is released; in all moments."

"All energy matrices that allow sacred water to be polluted

are sent into the Light and Sound to dissolve; in all moments."

"All complex energy matrices that allow sacred water to be polluted are dissolved into the Light and Sound; in all moments."

"All contracts with water pollution are nullified; in all moments."

"All vows and agreements with those that pollute sacred water are recanted; in all moments."

"All curses of water pollution are removed; in all moments."

"All blessings of water pollution are removed; in all moments."

"All strings, cords and ties with water pollution are severed; in all moments."

"All karmic ties with water pollution are dissolved; in all moments."

"All energy is withdrawn from those who pollute sacred water; in all moments."

"All pain, burden and limitations of water pollution are removed; in all moments."

"All fear, futility and unworthiness that water pollution causes is removed; in all moments."

"All loyalty to those who pollute sacred water is removed; in all moments."

"All anger, entitlement and illusion of separateness induced by water pollution is removed; in all moments."

"All resonating and emanating with water pollution is released; in all moments."

"All lack caused by water pollution is removed; in all moments."

"All disease caused by water pollution is removed; in all moments."

"All that those that poison sacred water have taken, is returned; in all moments."

"All wounds inflicted by water pollution are healed; in all moments."

"All desecration of sacred water is collapsed and dissolved; in all moments."

"All energy systems that have been compromised by water pollution are healed and repaired; in all moments."

"The sanctity of sacred water is restored; in all moments."

"All water of the planet is centered and empowered in purity; in all moments."

"All water of the planet is perpetually purified and honored with gratitude in all moments."

"All water on the planet resonates, emanates and is interconnected with all life in purity; in all moments."

"All the water of the planet is returned to purity; in all moments."

"All water of the planet resonates, emanates, and is interconnected with all life in gratitude and respect for its gift to the world; in all moments."

-Joy Love Abundance-

Self Esteem Marathon

One of the biggest problems with people is their lack of confidence in their own ability. It is because in so many lifetimes and experiences, we have been diminished, enslaved, imprisoned, used, sacrificed, tortured, humiliated, broken, beaten and abandoned, and scorned. We have adopted the belief that we are born in sin so that our very existence is contingent on performing great acts to overcome an innate flaw. The only way we can shine and still be acceptable is to be the best at being the most undeserving. It is a reverse play of the ego.

We have been taught to compete in life to win. But we are not at war with others. It has become an eternal battle that calls up unconscious memories when the battles were life and death.

Here are taps to help rekindle one's dynamic self:

"I release hating myself; in all moments."

"I release the belief that God hates me; in all moments."

"I release the guilt and trauma of hurting others; in all moments."

"I release the belief that God is punishing me; in all moments."

"I release the belief that I am damned; in all moments."

"I release the belief that I am a sinner; in all moments."

"I recant my vow of servitude; in all moments."

"I recant my vow of humility; in all moments."

"I recant my vow of self deprecation; in all moments."

"I recant my vow of self deprivation; in all moments."

"I recant my vow to not transcend; in all moments."

"I release sabotaging myself; in all moments."

"I release all the trauma of the past; in all moments."

"I release all the fear of the future; in all moments."

"I release the fear and trauma of being seen; in all moments."

"I release being invisible; in all moments."

"I release the fear of abusing power; in all moments."

"I release choosing power over love; in all moments."

"I release the fear and trauma of being separated from the herd; in all moments."

"I recant all vows and agreements I have made with myself; in all moments."

"I remove all curses that I have put on myself; in all moments."

"I remove all false beliefs I have been operating under; in all moments."

"I dissolve all karmic ties that I have tangled myself in; in all moments."

"I remove all the pain, burden and limitations I have put on myself; in all moments."

"I remove all the pain, burden, limitations that I have put on all others; in all moments."

"I take back all the joy, love, abundance, freedom, health, success, security, companionship, peace, life, wholeness, beauty, enthusiasm, spontaneity, contentment and enlightenment I have kept from myself; in all moments."

"I give back all that I have taken from all others; in all moments."

"I call back all my parts; in all moments."

"I make myself whole; in all moments."

"I repair and fortify my Wei Chi; in all moments."

"I am centered and empowered in Divine Love; in all moments."

"I happily and unabashedly share my gifts; in all moments."

If this exercise can help you share your abilities and feel the confidence that you deserve to feel, then you will be able to own that greatness that deep down we both know you feel. If you can do it for yourself, others will learn from watching you. Here is leading all to self-empowerment.

-Freedom Health Success-

Releasing Panic Attacks

I just finished facilitating an emergency session with someone who has suffered with panic attacks. They have been so bad that they have induced her to fainting. We have unpeeled many layers of the issues and right now, a huge event in her life where she will be the center of attention is bringing a lot of angst to the surface. It is a fertile place to release it and uncover the core issues.

In the session, she was having trouble breathing, which

makes sense because she is terrified of dying which she processes by losing consciousness (fainting).

Here are some taps that helped her and may help others:

"I release equivocating breathing as consciousness; in all moments."

"I release being separate from my breath; in all moments."

"I release the fear of being separated from my breath; in all moments."

"I release confusing being the center of attention as a precursor to death; in all moments."

"I release the fear of being separated from my consciousness; in all moments."

"I release fighting my own agreements; in all moments."

I release fighting myself; in all moments."

"I am centered in my own breath; in all moments."

"I surrender to my own agreements; in all moments."

"I accept myself; in all moments."

She had made an agreement with life. This life is her agreement. She sometimes senses it on the whole and it gets overwhelming. She has to slow herself down and realize that everything that comes to her is her agreement to life. She must remind herself that the trauma is a memory, not a looming future. By relaxing, and surrendering to the process of living, she is honoring her own agreements.

She performed the taps with me and wasn't aware of the shift they had created in her yet. So I asked her to put her fiance on the phone. The fear of having him talk to me shifted her intangible fear to a closer threat of exposure. I pushed the issue until she was able to bring all of herself into the problem at hand. Then I removed that threat by telling her never mind. She was so relieved that she relaxed and was pulled out of panic mode. Genius right?

If one person can do something, and we are all of the same make up, it makes sense that another person can do it as well. How many times have you witnessed someone sharing their gift and thought, *I could never do that.* The first primal thoughts that manifest within you should be, *yes I can do that! I want to do that. It may not be the same but it will be good!* This is what young children do.

If you go into a classroom of five-year-olds and ask them, "Who can draw?" most will raise their hands. If you ask them, "Who can sing?" most will raise their hands. If you ask them “Who can dance?” most will raise their hands. If you do that with a group of adults, maybe one or two will come forward. That is their ego getting in the way. Being afraid to be criticized is the ego. Being afraid of not being good enough is ego. We have been taught to compete in life to win. But we are not at war with others. It has become an eternal battle that calls up unconscious memories when the battles were life and death.

Release the Connection to Abusers

When a dog has been kept in a cage for a long time, it is difficult for them to come out. When they have been abused over a period of time, they naturally cower. This happens with people as well.

I can tell when someone has been abused. The internal cowering translates to the next life. It takes a lot of love and nurturing to undo the effect of abuse. It is easy to attract someone else to come in and take the role of an abuser if your energy says that you are used to being abused.

These taps can be a shortcut to release those energetic signals that say that one is comfortable with abuse.

(Say each statement three times while tapping on your head and say it a fourth time while tapping on your chest.)

"I release attracting abusers; in all moments."

"I recant all vows and agreements between myself and all the abusers; in all moments."

"I remove all curses between myself and all the abusers; in all moments."

"I dissolve all karmic ties between myself and all the abusers; in all moments."

"I remove all the pain, burden, limitations and programming that all abusers have put on me; in all

moments.”

"I remove all the pain, burden and limitations that I have put on all the abusers; in all moments.”

"I take back all the Joy, Love, Abundance, Freedom, Health, Success, Security, Companionship, Peace, Life, and Wholeness that all abusers have taken from me; in all moments.”

"I give back all the Joy, Love, Abundance, Freedom, Life, and Wholeness that I have taken from all abusers; in all moments.”

"I release resonating with all abusers; in all moments.”

"I release emanating with all abusers; in all moments.”

"I remove all abusers from my sound frequency; in all moments.”

"I remove all abusers from my Light body; in all moments.”

"I shift my paradigm from all abusers to joy, love, abundance, freedom, life, peace and wholeness; in all moments."

"I am centered in joy, love, abundance, freedom, life, peace and wholeness; in all moments.”

Negative Subliminal Message

If you think about it, associating a horrendous disease with the same color as innocent little girls is just another subtle way of diminishing women.

-Joy Love Abundance-

Healing the Wounded Sexuality

Recently I facilitated a session with a new client. She had no idea what to expect from a session, and I never know what a session is going to reveal.

I can tell a lot by a person's voice. Their sound frequency reveals so much. She seemed real open but there was a block like a huge brick wall between herself and her heart.

I perceived past live scenarios of her in a cult. The leader was really dynamic and larger than life. He was treated like a god by the members. She was a young girl and brought to his bed way too early in life. It was supposed to be an honor, so it set up a strange dichotomy in her in regards to sex.

She validated that she had sexual issues in this life that even her most patient husband could not help her get past.

In that past life, the leader would use her as a prop to teach young boys how to enjoy a woman. It was merely a thinly disguised demonstration to put the young girl in a degrading position. It thrilled him to do this. He pulled on one of her nipples in front of the boys to show them how the texture changed when it was touched. He instructed her to lay back and pulled back one of her labia to instruct the young boys how to enter her.

He invited them all to come touch her and encouraged then to poke inside her with their young fingers. She was instructed to feel honored in being chosen and yet the humiliation was inevitable. This is the dichotomy that was playing out in her present life and preventing her from enjoying her husband. Releasing her dynamics with the cult leader and the following taps are what we released during her session.

(Say each statement three times out loud while tapping on your head and say it a fourth time while tapping on your chest.)

"I release the trauma of being physically raped; in all moments."

"I release the trauma of being emotionally raped; in all moments."

"I release the trauma of being mentally raped; in all moments."

"I release confusing sex for power; in all moments."

"I release confusing sex for submission; in all moments."

"I release confusing sex for danger; in all moments."

"I release confusing sex for fear; in all moments."

"I release confusing sex for hate; in all moments."

"I release confusing sex for poverty; in all moments."

"I release selling sex for money; in all moments."

"I release confusing sex for manipulation; in all moments."

"I release confusing sex for slavery; in all moments."

"I release confusing sex for domination; in all moments."

"I release confusing sex for evil; in all moments."

"I release confusing sex for shame; in all moments."

"I release storing shame in my body, in all moments."

"I release being ashamed of myself; in all moments."

"I release making love to power; in all moments."

"I release confusing power for love; in all moments."

"I release defining sex as shameful; in all moments."

"I release defining sex as a sin; in all moments."

"I release using sex to feel worthy; in all moments."

"I release using sex to feel loved; in all moments."

"I release using sex to feel safe; in all moments."

"I release using sex to wield power; in all moments."

"I release associating pain with sex; in all moments."

"I release associating fear with sex; in all moments."

"I release confusing sex with devotion; in all moments."

"I release needing to give sex to prove loyalty; in all moments."

"I release confusing Love-making with rape; in all moments."

"I release the belief that sex is anything but loving and wonderful; in all moments."

"I recant all vows and agreements between myself and sex; in all moments."

"I remove all curses between myself and sex; in all moments."

"I sever all strings and cords between myself and sex; in all moments."

"I dissolve all karmic ties between myself and sex; in all moments."

"I remove all the pain, fear, shame, burdens, limitations and engrams that sex has put on me; in all moments."

"I take back all the dignity, joy, love, abundance, freedom, health success, security, companionship, peace, life, wholeness, beauty, enthusiasm, contentment, spirituality, enlightenment and confidence that sex has taken from me; in all moments."

"I release all sexual perversion; in all moments."

"I remove all masks, walls and armor between myself and intimate, joyful, trusting love-making; in all moments."

"I infuse joy, love, intimacy, trust and play into the sexual act; in all moments."

"I am centered and empowered in joyful, intimate, trusting love-making; in all moments."

After we released these issues, I encouraged her to surprise her husband in a sexy outfit. She said she wore them early in their relationship to keep him interested. I pointed out that she was using them as a form of manipulation. So now, wear the outfits as a gift for her husband and that will be shifting the experience to one of love.

Also, I told her to use the water-based markers and have her and her husband write on each other. I told her to allow him to write on all the parts where she felt shame in the past. By doing this he will be replacing the old experiences with love. She was to do the same to the parts of his body where she felt shame to touch. It is a conscious way to replace the old reactions with love. Then, of course, to shower together in play.

She was happy to do this exercise. I think in doing so, we have made a believer out of her husband of the energy work.

-Freedom Health Success-

Healing Female Energy

Recently, I allowed one of my clients to come to my home and worked with her in person. She is a dynamic advocate for women and operates with strong male energy. She has made it her purpose to empower female energy in all her friends. She is steadfast in dealing with all their imposed or self-inflicted imitations and works tirelessly at being an example of empowered female energy.

In her sessions, we took her to a time when female energy was revered as much as male energy. There were temples to groom the most gifted priestesses. They would be mated to the most powerful kings and would rule together. He, using his single-pointed directness as the kingdom's protector and she, using her expansive awareness to keep an overview of the kingdom and all its subtle needs.

Barbarian kings, who were jealous of the power that these elite kingdoms held, realized that they could use brute strength to break these noble allegiances by destroying the temples where the women were taught their skills. They bastardized the temples, raped and stole the women to perform their magic for them. The women were made mothers to these barbarian kings' children and it was demanded that they perform their magic. The women tried to pass their arts down to their children, but the customs were diluted until only the dance remained. The arousal was the kings' belief that their women were doing their magic. It was all they understood. If the men were aroused, they believed they had access to the priestesses' gifts. Many exotic dancers are trying to reclaim their insights through the dance and touching upon these past life experiences.

In a past life, my client was a man and she was tricked in helping the barbarian kings raid a sacred temple. He (she) immediately regretted it and was horrified with what transpired. She spent her lifetimes trying to rectify this transgression. In her present life session with me, we combed out many of her issues and guilt pertaining to female energy.

During her session, the phone rang. I don't usually answer calls when I am with someone but this time I was compelled to. I had the speaker on my phone turned on, so she was able to hear the call. It was a man who was following up about an order I placed. I could tell how wounded and in pain this man was. When I hung up, I asked her what she heard in his voice. She was crying and did not know why.

She realized in that moment it was not only women who suffered from the imbalance in male and female energy. It was men who suffered too. Her issue was not only with making amends to female energy. It was making amends to humanity. She realized that the plight of women is the plight that happens within all, not just those who happen to be incarnated as women. As women are empowered and embraced as enthusiastically and confidently as men in society, it heals all of humanity and elevates us all.

-Joy Love Abundance-

Frozen in Indifference

A dear friend of mine has been working with me for a couple years now. Every time an issue comes up for her, we will work through it to release any pain or angst it causes her. She has become so open and more loving and kind than she has been in all her life. She exudes contentment, humility and a sweet loving resolve. She even credits not needing high blood pressure medicine after 25 years of taking it with working with me.

Lately, she has been having a pain in her right leg. It is a deep issue and when we connect, I will assist her in discovering an underlying cause. It is not easy to look at our own issues. It is similar to cleaning house. Sometimes it is easier to clean a friend's house instead of our own. Many times it is easier to love and validate others instead of loving and validating ourselves. Instead we stifle our own cry for help.

Physical pain on some level is a cry for validation and love.

She has this one habit of diminishing the importance of events and situations for herself. It is a deep-seated way to prevent herself from being hurt. For example, if she is going to a special event, she will say something like, "I don't really care what I wear. I will just throw on the outfit I wore the last time." Or she will say, "It doesn't really matter. I will just have a few people over and put some food out. It will be good enough."

For the last couple of months, her leg has been hurting and she has been asking for my help. I have been assisting, but the pain has not been totally released. As we visited last night, a past life of hers opened up. I saw her as an animal in a metal trap. Her leg was half frozen off. She was retrieving food for her family and anxious to get back to them when she got caught in one of those claw metal traps. As excruciating as it was, the emotional pain of not getting home to her family and feeling her life body freeze and the life force slipping farther away from them left an emotional numbness in her. She showed this in the present life by diminishing the importance of special occasions to her.

This was the moment to address it. I shared with her the connection between her physical pain and this past life. She deflected and would not look at it. She was numb to it. She moved all too quickly to another subject about something unrelated and she used those words again, "I don't care." It was time to pin the emotional issue to its manifestation.

"You do too care. You do!" I took her by surprise. "Imagine your babies are waiting for you. They are hungry and your teats are full of milk. Your husband is alone at home with them and they are all waiting for you to be cozy and safe. But you are trapped in the cold metal jaw and freezing to death not able to get to them. You know they will most likely starve without you and think you have abandoned them. You care!"

She was taken aback and cried a deep soulful cry. If there were no connection to the scenario I had just painted, the sobs would not have continued like they did.

Here are some taps that helped as well:

I release being frozen in indifference; in all moments."

"I release the trauma of freezing to death; in all moments."

"I release the guilt and trauma of abandoning my family; in all moments."

"I forgive myself; in all moments."

Her husband had trapped animals in his youth. She was able to compartmentalize this as being okay. After the sobbing, we visualized the scenario that I saw and freed her in the trapped body. We poured incredible love into its little body. We changed the story of it to undo the emotional scar it left. We also visualized freeing all the animals that were ever trapped and killed in such a ruthless way. We poured love and healing into them all and the whole scenario.

DMSO

There is a natural miracle substance that exists that is so AMAZING that the FDA doesn't want you to know about it because it will revolutionize self-healing. I learned about it in the early eighties. I was a member of a secret metaphysical group. The leader, who was a high priestess reincarnated, wrote about it in one of her books. Way back then, it was being blocked from passing FDA standards. That was when I was naive enough to think that the FDA cared about the wellbeing of the consumer.

But now with all the reemerging awareness and the realization that the FDA is in the pockets of the drug companies, I have rediscovered it. I had forgotten it existed. But an amazing client of mine told me about it. I mentioned to her how amazing MSM was and she told me that MSM was basically a very diluted version of DMSO.

If you research it, you will read all these terrible things about it. How dangerous it is to take. But as I am aware of the real cautions, I am also aware of all the side effects that are mentioned on the commercials for sanctioned drugs. I got an enthusiastic nudge to try it.

What people may not know about me is that when I was in my early twenties, I was driving from college to my part time job and a drunk driver jackknifed my car as I was waiting for a light. I was immediately pulled out of my body and when I returned to it, there was a crowd of people around my car. They were afraid to come close because they thought I was dead. The car was pushed over four lanes of traffic into a glass showcase of an ice cream store, bounced off and flipped around.

I was pulled out with the Jaws of Life. I lost partial usage of my left arm and felt "off" after that. But I wasn't aware of the true extent of the damage. When I went through massage therapy school, one of the perceptive energy workers sensed a spinal chord injury. It wasn't until I got a tens unit that runs electric current through the body that I realized how much feeling I had lost.

What I was told by my Spirit Guides was that I should have been paralyzed in that crash. But that wouldn't have served my purpose in this life. And now, as I am emerging from my camouflage, I have rediscovered the DMSO again. It has been known to regenerate nerve damage.

I hadn't realized how much my body was in pain except I have been having trouble walking and getting around. The legs stiffen up whenever I sit. But that is changing now with the DMSO. I started taking it cautiously because of all I have read about it. Its components draw it through the tissue membrane of the body so it is best to not have any chemicals of any kind on the skin. Also, it can cause a reaction with medications. But I don't take any medications, so I didn't experience any problems in taking it.

I read that it is good to apply it in pure magnesium oil

because it will draw both it and the magnesium deep into the tissue. On my first day of taking it, I experienced the euphoria of youth. It was as if there was a shroud of depression that I never acknowledged that was suddenly lifted. I have been in joy since I started taking it and am enjoying the experience of having twinges of nerve pain as my body reawakens. It seems to bring a glow to the skin and a feeling of deep contentedness. I am so grateful to have found it again.

The FDA is trying to ban this product. I am hoping that this doesn't happen. I am sharing so those who are awakening will have this tool to regain their wellbeing and their ability to discern. There are cautions to follow in taking it. It is a dynamic tool in wellbeing and it seems to be a basic building block of nature so I feel more connected to organic life by taking it.

Please do your research. Please use with caution. Please listen to your inner direction. It may not be for someone whose body is laced with medications. It may try to detox the sanctioned poisons from your body too quickly. I am telling you about it because you deserve to know that there are options. There are always ways to forge on for the betterment of all.

-Joy Love Abundance-

Deep Chakra Cleansing

A new client asked me if I could facilitate a chakra cleansing for her. I obliged. What was interesting is when I tuned into her, there seemed to be a different emotion "plugging up" each chakra. What follows is the taps we used to clear each chakra.

We used a tap to clear each of the different aspects of an individual. We cleared their physical, emotional, causal (body that stores the Akashic records of past lives and mental bodies.) We cleared all the chakras including the one above the head and one below the feet.

When you do these taps, realize that you are clearing each chakra, starting at the one above the head. Each chakra is cleared here on different levels. The tap that says "being" is clearing on a physical level. The tap that says "feeling" is clearing on the emotional level. The one that says engram is clearing on the causal level and the one that mentions "beliefs" is clearing the chakra at the mental level.

The last tap is one that infuses the tap with higher awareness.

(Say each statement three times while tapping on your head and say it a fourth time while tapping on your chest. Pause before “in all moments.”)

Soul Star Chakra

“I release being hopeless; in all moments.”

"I release feeling hopeless; in all moments."

"I remove all engrams of hopelessness; in all moments."

"I release the belief that things are hopeless; in all moments."

"I infuse knowingness into my whole beingness; in all moments."

"I am centered and empowered in knowingness; in all moments."

Crown Chakra

I release being trapped; in all moments

I release feeling trapped; in all moments."

I remove all engrams of being trapped; in all moments."

I release the belief that I am trapped; in all moments."

I infuse absolute freedom into my whole beingness; in all moments."

"I am centered and empowered in absolute freedom; in all moments."

Third Eye

"I release being diminished; in all moments."

"I release feeling diminished; in all moments."

“I remove all engrams of being diminished; in all moments.”

“I release the belief that I am diminished; in all moments.”

“I infuse empowerment into my whole beingness; in all moments.”

"I am centered and empowered in being totally empowered; in all moments.”

Throat Chakra

“I release having no voice; in all moments.”

“I release feeling like I have no voice; in all moments.”

“I remove all engrams of having no voice; in all moments.”

“I release the belief that I have no voice; in all moments.”

“I infuse speaking my truth into my whole beingness; in all moments.”

"I am centered and empowered in speaking my truth; in all moments.”

Heart Chakra

“I release being afraid; in all moments.”

“I release feeling afraid; in all moments.”

“I remove all engrams of fear; in all moments.”

"I release the belief that I am afraid; in all moments."

"I infuse confidence into my whole beingness; in all moments."

"I am centered and empowered in absolute confidence; in all moments."

Solar Plexus

"I release being enslaved; in all moments."

"I release feeling enslaved; in all moments."

"I remove all engrams of being enslaved; in all moments."

"I release the belief that I am enslaved; in all moments."

"I infuse personal freedom into my whole beingness; in all moments."

"I am centered and empowered in personal freedom; in all moments."

Sacral Chakra

"I release being weak; in all moments."

"I release feeling weak; in all moments."

"I remove all engrams of being weak; in all moments."

"I release the belief that I am weak; in all moments."

"I infuse strength into my whole beingness; in all moments."

"I am centered and empowered in being strong; in all

moments."

Root Chakra

"I release being unbalanced; in all moments."

"I release feeling unbalanced; in all moments."

"I remove all engrams of imbalance; in all moments."

"I release the belief that I am unbalanced; in all moments."

"I infuse balance into my whole beingness; in all moments."

"I align and balance all my bodies; in all moments."

Earth Star

"I release being disconnected; in all moments."

"I release feeling disconnected; in all moments."

"I remove all engrams of being disconnected; in all moments."

"I release the belief that I am disconnected; in all moments."

"I infuse connection to Source into my whole beingness; in all moments."

"I am centered and empowered in connection to Source; in all moments."

Being a Good Person

Sometimes being a good person is more than just mouthing words of encouragement that others want to hear. Sometimes it means advocating for someone who others would prefer to shun. Sometimes it is having compassion for an issue when others would prefer to sweep it under the rug. Sometimes it is taking the unfavorable stance, not to prove a point, but because there are real people with real feelings and real problems to factor in. Sometimes it may entail being unpopular. But are you going to think of yourself as a good person, or are you going to be one?

Some people are lonely and want to fit in. Some people are suffering with a dilemma and trying to maneuver through it. Many are desperately trying to make sense of their life, society, God, and their place in the mix of it. Some just want to turn off the barrage of thoughts and emotional angst that seem to string their existence together.

Did you know it is illegal in some states to say you can heal? It makes sense because of all the abuse that will come from that statement. But it is legal to administer drugs that have such side effects that are more horrific and devastating than any condition. It is legal to medicate children and be dependent on medications for life. It is legal to poison our environment as long as the poisons fly under the radar.

To me holding a positive intention for someone is a form of healing. In that respect, I am a healer because that is my intention for all. So instead of being respected for what I do and how I help people, I am not considered more than a good person.

I have been consciously helping others my whole life. That seems to be my purpose for being here. I have accepted that I just don't fit into society or a niche or any group. But I continue to help others. Even though I know that after I help someone they are going to be embarrassed to tell others about it. I know when someone wants to see me, it is because they need some kind of help even though they really sincerely think they are being genuine in wanting to see or talk to me for me. I also realize that when I go out of my way to assist someone who is crying out in pain that they will later scoff at my help, ignore me, or attribute the help to some other variable.

I will continue to be a good person even if I know I will be ostracized, used, unappreciated or undervalued. That is my agreement with Love. I will Love even though it is not returned, and I will do what I can to make this world a better place for those I see suffering. This is the bar I have set for my personal integrity. I encourage others to be a good person, not because there is a short-term pay off, but because easing the dis-ease of others is the ultimate reward.

Here are some ways to be a good person:

- Do what you agree to do.
- Say only kind things about others.
- Paint only uplifting scenarios for others to walk into
- Let others outshine you.
- Acknowledge the individual plight of all you encounter.
- Listen with your heart and answer with your heart.
- Allow people to feel good about themselves.
- Do what you can to assist others without coming out of your center.
- Allow people their dreams.
- See others lives from their vantage point, not yours.
- Allow room for others to grow and change direction.
- Expect nothing from others.
- Ask yourself what would Love do?
- Do what Love would do until you become Love itself.

-Joy Love Abundance-

Activate Your Healing Empowerment

"I release demonizing the Healer; in all moments."

"I release mistrust of natural Healing; in all moments."

"I release only accepting Healing through synthetic means; in all moments."

"I release confusing Healers as charlatans; in all moments."

"I release denying my own Healing abilities; in all moments."

"I release the fear of being demonized for my Healing abilities; in all moments."

"I release doubting what is possible; in all moments."

"I release the need to quantify Healing; in all moments."

"I release the need to diminish Healing; in all moments."

"I release confusing the physiology of Healing with magic or the dark arts; in all moments."

"I release categorizing Healers as quacks, frauds, flakes or psychos; in all moments."

"I remove all negative programming I have in regards to Healers; in all moments."

"I release giving my power over to synthetic means; in all moment"

"I release entrusting my health to synthetic means; in all moments."

"I shift my paradigm from synthetic means to natural Healing; in all moments."

"I transcend all synthetic means; in all moments."

"I activate my own Healing empowerment; in all moments."

"I am centered and empowered in my own Healing empowerment; in all moments."

6: LEADING FROM THE HEART

Upgrade to the Understanding of a Four Year Old

I imagine the generations that survived during the war. The people quietly living lives of meaning with the whole world crumbling around them, raising children, providing for loved ones and seeing each other through with no sense of when the madness would end.

I don't imagine that they sat around and perpetuated the negativity of the situation by talking about it incessantly and how awful it was. I don't think they wanted to acknowledge the madness in which they were living. Perhaps their greatest survival tool was looking for glimmers of hope where they were given little evidence of it.

The same powers that enjoyed conflict back then, try to sweep the land and kick up controversy and hate to pull the masses into that whole experience again. Those who did not get enough of the "excitement" in a past life may be leading the brigade this lifetime.

Notice how experienced, battle fatigued veterans are not over zealous for war? Many of us incarnated this lifetime are battle fatigued. In fact, the majority of us would really like to experience the flip side of the experience. We would like to dip our toe into the perpetual presence of Universal peace. That is an intention worth feeding.

The psychic band of power is always at play it seems, goading us to stand up for our rights in a peripheral way. They use the best fear mongering that propaganda can buy. They have the best tactics of sectioning us up in demographics and prodding us to defend these imaginary divisions to death. They have programmed us and conditioned generation after generation to the affect that we have lost the ability to question or to implement common sense.

The truth of the matter is that if the powers that incited us to war really wanted peace, we would have it. That is not their true purpose. Their true purpose is to immerse us in infighting and reacting in fear so much that we lose sight of our unalienable rights: life, liberty and the pursuit of happiness. These are not being stripped away from us by the enemy on the other side of the world. These are being dwindled down by our own government and institutions that we trust regardless of what area of the world where we live.

Our best defense from becoming a world of puppets supporting a global police state is to think and discern for ourselves, and question every group that we have given blind allegiance to. So many of us are like the adult child whose independence is stunted by an over strict parent. It is a distortion that everyone can see except the parent and child.

It is disturbing to hear anyone in a position of authority salivate over using power. But what is even more disturbing is watching so many competent individuals stand by and witness such a thing and do nothing to address it. People need to understand that the media and anything with mass audience is polluted and distorted towards power.

Power enjoys razing things to the ground. Power enjoys creating devastation and seeing innocence suffer. Power considers individuals as a necessary sacrifice. In fact, the more emotion that power can exploit through the suffering of individuals, the more it is fed. Need an example? All those videos of the soldiers returning to surprise their child in an emotional reunion at their school event. We all cry and love them. Who gets angry that the parent and child were separated to begin with? These videos feed the cogs of power that have created the pain in the first place. I refuse to watch them. The participants don't realize their tender reunions are used to normalize a heartbreaking separation.

All this emotion feeds warmongers. Who is excited about joining the military? New adults that are so hungry for opportunity and adventure that their hormones are bursting to sign up. It is no different than the young girl being deeply devoted to the first man who makes her feel like a woman. The military seduces our young people in a similar way and yet that is fine. In fact, I may get attacked ruthlessly for speaking against such a well-oiled propaganda machine as the military.

That support of the military that we see propagated by our precious football teams is paid advertisement by the military. It hits people when they are all immersed in the sportsmanship of our favorite game and gets us to believe that we are all on the same page about the military. It is like getting a husband to agree to something by buttering him up. That is what is happening with war being advertised during football.

But someone has to crack through the facade. And you are not seeing truth happen either in the media or in any group at all. Because all groups are a finely woven interplay of different means of robbing the individuals of their God given rights of empowerment and discernment. Anyone who subscribes to a mentality and conditioning that was implemented during the Dark Ages is still living in the Dark Ages.

I am not trying to desecrate what others hold sacred. But if it leads us to policing each other's bodies and sending each other's husbands and children to war, then it needs to be questioned. People have to stop romanticizing God as someone who wants to degrade individuals and be worshiped. If you think about it, that sounds more like the political power brokers who we are all seeing wield power in current events. Can God not do better than that?

Can we not raise the bar on how we perceive the Source of all life? Can we not see it past gender or needing its ego stroked? Can we not see it loving individuals with at least as much kindness and unconditional compassion as a mother loves her child? When the systemic diminishing of woman happened during the Dark Ages, so were these altruistic qualities stripped from our understanding of God's virtue.

The fear and threats of perpetual hell are what we have been deduced to by the power plays that use our devotion to the divine to diminish and control us. We are, if not in hell, at least in a purgatory of which the Bible once wrote. Purgatory is earth. When they stripped all references to past lives out of the Bible, they also stripped out the belief in purgatory because they realized that some day we would figure it out. I was four when I did. It is time for humanity to upgrade to the understanding of a four year old.

I am like you. I don't like to offend. I have been polite and non-confrontational while the rest of the world stumbled on truth of its own accord. But with each crop of new adults, truth has been dumbed down even more. Young people don't even realize that a few short decades ago, you could actually get clear facts reported on the news with no slant or guile. News reporters were mandated to stay neutral and were fired if they wavered. The younger generations may never realize truth unadulterated or free of corruption.

The only way some people will ever know truth or be able to discern it for themselves is if people stop being polite and start speaking truth as their native tongue again. As it is now, truth has gone the ways of the Latin language and is only taught as an intellectual exercise. People must get over their need to be polite or over the fear of being bullied for speaking truth. Anyone, who is brave enough to do so, is protected by the Ancient Ones in sharing truth and advocating for those who are so lost in rhetoric or programming that they will spit at you for your efforts.

Individuals sharing truth is how this world will be salvaged.

Going along with the group consensus in any way that diminishes others or propagates fear is a desecration of truth. Talking about how miserable current affairs are, without offering a resolve or a way to empower others, is merely indulging the power mongers with free press. We are all better than this. So many may resonate with this message and yet unless they share truth and add their goodness to the mix, truth will be like damp kindling.

Look at our commercials and you will see glimmers of truth. Don't be fooled that this is perpetuating truth. It has merely ensconced it in a sound bite to perpetuate the enslavement to materialism. Advertising collects what we hold dear to feed back to us merely to hook us back in. Advertisers use pieces of fish on their hook to catch bigger fish. They troll for what humanity cares about only to hook them back into mass appeal. Please stop falling for this.

People who deem themselves spiritual beyond approach will talk about free will to leave others to suffer in ignorance. This has created a systemic apathy. It has also created a glass ceiling on our spiritual efforts. One has to wonder if even the most profound group teachings have not been railroaded by a male agenda, which has left most of those who feel advanced, duped in a most dubious way.

People would have free will if they weren't all sinking in quicksand. It is cruel to sit on the sidelines while someone is drowning and lecture them on having free will. Pull them up out of the mud first, clean them up, and give them a meal and then when they are on a level playing ground, leave them to free will.

If the spiritual community feels that their teachings are beyond reproach, I challenge them to challenge anything that they have been told outwardly and direct themselves back to the more subjective inner realms for an upgrade. The Ancient Ones are using all those that are open to truth to break the mass enslavement that humanity has been pummeled with.

If anyone is still concerned with a particular stance in any way and is butting heads with others to perpetuate an agenda, they are still immersed in the power plays at a subtle level. But if one is tuned into the suffering that happens beyond their station or privileges in this life, then perhaps they are more tapped into truth than their inflated ego of self-importance.

Those who are tapped into truth will be free to incarnate into better conditions. Those who perpetuate an agenda, no matter how adamant they are that they have a direct line to the grand poobah, will need to incarnate back into the conditions that they have contributed to creating. This is the free will that so many use to quantify an arrogant stance. The latter is indeed a choice that so many are in need of correcting.

-Joy Love Abundance-

The Brilliance of Your Form

You are way too magnificent and expansive to focus all your attention on a pimple on your face.

Why do you define yourself by a little extra girth on your body?

Don't you realize that it represents all the pain and struggle and sacrifice you have endured just to exist here?

How dare you let anyone shame you?

How dare you shame yourself with silly words like fat or ugly?

Don't you realize that you are made of the same stuff as the heavens? Even the Gods?

Who cares what shoes you wear?

Who cares if your purse matches your dress?

Who made these rules?

Was it someone who has watched over your struggle through the eons and has blessed you every step of the way?

Or is it a force that shames, coerces and manipulates all the beauty of creation into conformity?

Which voice do you listen to when you lay your head down at night?

Or when you are doing your best to care for your loved ones?

Or merely trying to get through yet another cycle of the day?

Are you blessing the world with your greatness?

Or are you cursing yourself with personal admonishment?

There is no enemy coming for you.

There is no one that is making it their mission to destroy you.

That is all done by you with your petty thoughts and haunting beliefs.

It's okay to discharge that inner taskmaster of the duty of admonishing you.

No one will rebuke you for showing kindness to yourself.

Yet all of the heavens will sing at this one act of sweet rebellion.

When you finally realize, finally understand the sacred trust you are given, to love all of life, through yourself—

Then you unlock the mystery of all of life: That you are the doorway to the infinite.

When you belittle yourself, you shut the door on the wonders of the Universe.

Awakening entails foregoing the constant barrage of the self-deprecating onslaught.

It is to be at peace with all the flecks and inflections in your perfect wonder,

And revel in them as they catch and reflect the light.

As you unabashedly celebrate the brilliance of your form, in dance.

-Freedom Health Success-

Creating a Pattern of Kindness

The world can't as easily mend with everyone withholding their gifts to sell an agenda. That is what male energy does. One has to be so in love with their purpose that they give effortlessly as much as possible. This doesn't mean being a doormat for others to take. It means finding a balance between giving freely and also maintaining one's own integrity of service. I work at being an example of that.

I have business savvy people tell me that I give too much away. That it prevents people from needing my services and works against my own business. But I am not in this world to be a business. I am in this world to uplift as many souls as possible. I believe this is done by showing them the balance between their own empowerment and what they have to give to others. If I left people in need, that would be doing what male energy has done all throughout modern history. That is why the world was left in such need.

It is up to all people to embrace their own female energy, give love and thrive with a passion of sisterhood for all life. We are so close to making an incredible shift in bringing the world from needing to thriving. It is done with every individual who has cracked the code on both giving and receiving, from the depth of their own goodness.

Self-denial, martyrdom, victim consciousness are all things of the past. It is time for all aware and awakening souls to figure out how to make every scenario a win-win, to stop indulging in "them versus us" mode, and to create a world that is patterned after love and kindness and not after power and conquest. We do this when we practice kind, giving principles in our own little corner of the world and send them out like loving ebbs of gifting for all to learn from and embrace.

-Joy Love Abundance-

I Am Alone Today

There is no one in my life that wishes to spend time with me today. No one really cares about me. I don't matter. I must be so annoying to be around that no one wants to even extend human kindness to me. It is irrelevant to everyone here whether I exist or not. I must be hard to Love. I don't even attract life partners because there is nothing attractive about me.

These are the thoughts that the human consciousness bombards me with. These are the thoughts that induce pain and dredge up old instances of injury and indignation. But I choose to turn down the channel on such silly notions. I listen to my heart.

This is what the heart tells me:

Being with people is a distraction. The Universe is strengthening your capacity to be imbued with love by not having you believe that it originates from other people.

You give so much of yourself. You need to pour that love into the world and not waste it on those who feel entitled to it.

You are being blessed to have all the humans pushed out of your life so that you can develop your ability to love other species of life and have an intimate relationship with life itself.

You are too aware to be trapped in the conventions of social culture. If the Universe left it to you, you would be distracted all the days of your life trying to please and placate others.

Everything that you are given daily in life lessons and spiritual awareness becomes a part of you even when you cross over. You are rich and abundant beyond compare in the spiritual realms. Others are starving for your spiritual gifts. Don't waste energy or momentum by focusing on those around you who don't see your greatness.

Isn't life a thorough teacher to provide you with a buffer from people adoring you? All those around you who don't see your greatness assist you so well in staying focused on the sanctity of the moment and not being distracted by the illusions.

No one can see you because so few people see truth, beauty and love in the world. You resonate so closely to truth, beauty and love that you have indeed become invisible to the average human.

Your Spiritual light is very bright. For some humans, it blinds them. In this world of illusion, the way they respond to that is by being put off by you. But that is only more reason to have compassion for them.

All the security and material comforts that humans strive to accrue are only their limited attempts to own the intangible gifts that come so readily to you.

The Universe is gifting you with isolation so it can help you drop out of the illusion of the moment and become alive, aware and expansive in the true interconnection of all.

God is not punishing you. You are being gifted with great insight and lasting spiritual capabilities every moment. By ignoring the mind's taunting, you are awakening to the sanctity of all life.

You and your gifts are so important to the world that you are not allowed to waste this existence being caught up in the illusion of the day and the pettiness of man.

Thanksgiving is a day to teach others as a group how to be grateful and how to interconnect with others. You have already learned these lessons, so you do not need to go through the tedious lesson plans that other humans need.

Wanting what other humans have is like wishing to go back to kindergarten because you like coloring. You create masterpieces my friend. Use your abilities to do so.

These are some of the things that my heart tells me. It also tells me that I am being used as an example to show people how the shift from human consciousness to spiritual consciousness is done. It also tells me that there are those out there who need to hear this. This is what their hearts have been telling them as well. Those who need to hear this will find this message and realize that they are loved and important in the scheme of life. They matter and are more dear than all the home spun celebrations can convey.

Please get a sense of how important you are to life and of the transcendence process from the mundane to the dynamic. Use any pain you may endure as a benchmark of the greatness of your true self. May you realize your true worth in the expansion of consciousness. You matter. You really do. You are loved beyond compare. You really are.

Some will argue that they can't matter because they don't

outshine others in this life. You are not paying attention. It is a lie of the human consciousness that you must be great on the backs of others. That is how male energy has programmed the world.

But female energy embraces greatness as a sisterhood where all are happiest when everyone is at their best. That is the reality of where human awareness is headed. By dropping out of the lies of the illusion, you can plug into the expansiveness of the ultimate truth. As one succeeds in the true sense, we all succeed.

Here is to the success of the human species to transcend. I love you all. Every single one of you. Because I can. And that is a gift that human loneliness has afforded me. I would not trade that for anything.

-Joy Love Abundance-

The Energetic Effects of Swearing

I had one beautiful Goddess client go through the process of enlightenment simply by doing the taps and sessions with me and to forego using swearing as a means of communicating and defacing the caliber of her own vibration. It is a way that male energy interjects its ugly influence into our speech and interconnection with other beautiful Goddesses. It makes us believe we are being effective, but we are dinging and pitting the pristine divine from within. It is a systemic way that the ugly aspect of male energy immerses itself into us. Swearing is a form of rape to female energy.

-Freedom Health Success-

Random Empowerment

(Say each statement three times while tapping on your head and say it a fourth time while tapping on your chest.)

"I drop the drama; in all moments."

"I recant my vow of martyrdom; in all moments."

"I recant my vow of poverty; in all moments."

"I nullify all contracts with all users; in all moments."

"I remove all curses on my female lineage; in all

moments.”

"I release the genetic propensity to be diminished; in all moments.”

-Joy Love Abundance-

Insecurities

When I was younger, I was one of those people who apologized to everyone around me. It was like I was apologizing for existing. I was saying, "I am sorry," all the time. It is humorous to me that I have become so direct, due to the energy work, and offend people through the process.

I used to want people to reassure me. Reassure me that I was good enough. I would fish for reassurance with anyone who was kind to me. It is the same way a love-starved dog will go to anyone just to seek approval. I never felt comfortable in my skin. I could feel the actual shame that was layered between myself and everyone else. It felt similar to a blush and was permanent.

I never really complained or talked about my problems because I knew no one was interested. But I did obsess when someone was kind to me and relived that experience over and over as a way to feel happiness. It was an escape for me to fantasize about something nice happening to me or someone liking me. So I understand how much of life can be wasted in this state.

Imagine having no sense of self, desperately wanting to experience love, having acute sensitivities and being immersed in dysfunction with the added camouflage of people believing that you had it together because you were pretty and had some intelligence. This may be a lot of people's experience in varying degrees. That is the whole point.

My whole life has been a field study in gaining a deep understanding for those stuck in their private hells. It is part of the reason why I understand what a person truly needs. When I am not sympathetic, it is because I know in that moment that sympathy will not be effective.

When one sympathizes with someone, they are agreeing with a particular viewpoint that further meshes a person into that unfavorable situation. It is like gluing the experience more strongly into the true self. When I am harsh with people, I am getting the putting knife out and removing old wallpaper from them. Sometimes it has been up so long that it feels like part of the person. It will feel painful or unkind. But it is an effective tool to assist the person in being free.

Their ego will be so identified with the situation that it will feel like I am hurting it and it will not want anything to do with me. The psyche will interpret that rawness that has been exposed as having their feelings hurt. Feelings should be hurt. The more fragile they are, the more they should be pulled from the person who wants to be more free.

Feelings are so low on the survival scale. Avoiding feelings to the emotions is like avoiding work and exercise to the physical body. Also, people will hide behind the facade of being nice. They will have this disconnect between their behavior and self-awareness. I have been fortunate to be able to observe the bully mentality in a few specimens. They really aren't aware that they are affecting people in such a way. They really believe that they are maligned and are the victim in life.

So here are a few taps that will help with that internal struggle with self-worth and self-esteem. (Say each statement three times out loud while tapping on your head and say it a fourth time while tapping on your chest.)

"I release apologizing for existing; in all moments."

"I release the need to make excuses; in all moments."

"I release perpetually defending myself; in all moments."

"I release needing reassurance; in all moments."

"I release seeking reassurance; in all moments."

"I release using reassurance to validate my existence; in all moments."

"I release confusing sympathy for love; in all moments."

"I release seeking sympathy; in all moments."

"I release being immersed in the quest for sympathy; in all moments."

"I release being surrounded by dysfunction; in all moments."

"I withdraw all my energy from all unworthy thoughts, feelings and deeds; in all moments."

"I release being a bully; in all moments."

"I release bullying others; in all moments."

"I release protecting the pain body at all costs; in all moments."

"I make space in this world for a confident awareness of self; in all moments."

"I remove all blockages to having a confident awareness of self; in all moments."

"I stretch my capacity to having a confident awareness of self; in all moments."

"I am centered and empowered in a loving confident awareness of self; in all moments."

God Speed to Your Goal

(Say each statement three times out loud while tapping on your head and say it a fourth time while tapping on your chest.)

"I make space in this world to ___________; in all moments."

"I remove all blockages to ____________; in all moments."

"I stretch my capacity to ______________; in all moments."

"I am worthy and deserve to ____________; in all moments."

"I release believing ______________ is too good to be true; in all moments."

"I open all portals to _______________; in all moments."

"I walk into the reality of _____________; in all moments."

"I collapse and dissolve all portals to disappointment and unfavorable results; in all moments."

"I infuse ____________ into my Light Frequency and Sound Emanation; in all moments."

Redefining Motherhood

Today, I facilitated a session with a young woman contemplating motherhood. She had many reservations, but they manifested as one mass confusion. The first thing that she would not admit to herself was that although she loved her husband, it was not a story book romance. Their relationship didn't reach the depth of fairytale romances. She was concerned about being connected for life to her husband as the father of her baby.

When I tuned in, I knew that she was harboring all the feelings about motherhood. But the baby that she was carrying was a true fairytale love. Her husband was the perfect father that would give this baby what he needed. This perspective reassured her.

The next issue was all these dynamics with her mother. She did not want to be annoyed with the baby like she was annoyed with her mother her whole life. She also didn't want to be like her mother. She identified negative traits with motherhood. I led her through a series of taps that brought some relief. But then more disturbing layers were revealed.

She described the feeling of being led through her life and losing control. The imagery of a past life emerged. She was being led to slaughter. Slowly and methodically she was moving closer and closer to her horrific death. There was no compassion, there was no kindness, just a methodical bludgeoning. This is the feeling that was being subliminally evoked every time she reached a major milestone in her life. She was correlating each event as a step closer to a horrific outcome. Motherhood was just another one of those steps.

When I helped her release this correlation, I inadvertently coughed. She told me that when I coughed, she had a strange tingling on the roof of her mouth. She was getting a sense of the imagery that I saw when I coughed. She was a newborn. She was unwanted, maybe because she was born a girl. She was put in a burlap bag at birth and taken out to the pond and drowned. It made her confuse birth with death and death with love. When she learned about this lifetime, it made her realize why she got freaked out when she thought about the amniotic sac. In her baby body, she confused the burlap sac with the amniotic sac.

As she was releasing these old engrams, images of many mother's day cards with wonderful sayings were running through my perception. It was as if a higher definition of motherhood was being downloaded into her. She felt much lighter. It was like untangling confusion and peeling off layers of trauma at the same time. The baby will now open her up to a love she has not experienced in so many of her lifetimes. It will almost be a means to actualize all the work we have done together and for her to truly and deeply experience an incredible, ethereal love.

Here are some of the taps on motherhood:

(Say each statement three times out loud while tapping on

your head and say it a fourth time while tapping on your chest.)

"I release defining motherhood as controlling; in all moments."

"I release defining motherhood as needy; in all moments."

"I release defining motherhood as negative; in all moments."

"I release defining motherhood as being the enemy; in all moments."

"I release the fear of becoming my mother; in all moments."

"I release the fear of being hated; in all moments."

"I release the fear of losing my freedom; in all moments."

"I release the fear of letting my baby down; in all moments."

"I release defining motherhood as imprisonment; in all moments."

"I release correlating motherhood with looming death; in all moments."

"I release the fear of being trapped by motherhood; in all moments."

"I recant all vows and agreements between myself and

motherhood; in all moments."

"I remove all curses between myself and motherhood; in all moments."

"I dissolve all karmic ties between myself and motherhood; in all moments."

"I remove all the pain, burden, limitations, and engrams that motherhood has put on me; in all moments."

"I take back all the Joy, Love, Abundance, Freedom, Health, Life and Wholeness that motherhood has taken from me; in all moments."

"I redefine Motherhood as Joy, Love, Abundance, Freedom, Health Life and Wholeness; in all moments."

-Freedom Health Success-

Dear Mom,

I'm tired of all the cards

That tell of a Mother's care

How especially thoughtful they are

And how their Love's so rare

They tell of deep devotion

A Divinity that's True...

But Mom they tell half of it

Because they don't know you

It's not the things you gave me,

Though those were real nice too

It's more the things you taught me

To help my Love shine through

Like treating people equal

Not thinking I am best

And loving those who don't love me

Is my best defense

You taught me what is real

And what is just pretense

To treat someone as special

While ignoring all the rest

So Mom

Thank you for the freedom

For the Love and Care

Thank you for the wisdom

That in others is sometimes rare

And as we walk the path of Life

If our Missions keep us apart

Know you are alive in my memories

And Dancing in my Heart.

7: RELATIONSHIPS

Changing Our Agreement with Society

We are not helpless dupes of society. We make up society. Our voice, feelings, beliefs, opinions and heart are added in the mix of what society entails. Just because we don't scream as loud to get our own way doesn't mean our truth is less valid.

Please do these taps as a way of uplifting the group consciousness of all of society. We must sever old agreements with it so as to formulate new and healthy interactions with each other where all individuals are valued, the quality of life is precious, freedom is a reality instead of a point of rhetoric and truth, justice and kindness prevail. Doing these taps is a silent way of claiming your own effectiveness.

(Say each statement three times out loud while continuously tapping on the top of your head at the crown chakra and say it a fourth time while tapping on your chest.)

"I declare myself a surrogate for humanity in doing these taps; in all moments."

"I release being an unwitting member of society; in all moments."

"I release the belief that I have no power in society; in all

moments."

"I release losing myself in society; in all moments."

"I release the fear of being rejected by society; in all moments."

"I release being a scapegoat of society; in all moments."

"I release being a scapegoat for society; in all moments."

"I release being demonized by society; in all moments."

"I release being ostracized by society; in all moments."

"I remove all vivaxes between myself and society; in all moments."

"I remove all tentacles between myself and society; in all moments."

"I send all energy matrices into the light that immerse society in negativity; in all moments."

"I send all energy matrices into the light that use society to control others; in all moments."

"I send all energy matrices into the light that use society to create a disconnectedness; in all moments."

"I remove all engrams that society has put in me; in all moments."

"I remove all forms of control that society has instilled in me; in all moments."

"I recant all vows and agreements between myself and society; in all moments."

"I remove all curses and blessings between myself and society; in all moments."

"I sever all strings and cords that society has put on me; in all moments."

"I dissolve all karmic ties between myself and society; in moments"

"I remove all the pain, burden, limitations and illusion of separateness that society has put on me; in all moments."

"I strip all of society of all its lies; in all moments."

"I strip all of society of its control; in all moments."

"I remove all masks, walls, armor, facade and illusion from society; in all moments."

"I take back all that society has taken from me; in all moments."

"I withdraw all my energy from society; in all moments."

"I render my allegiance to society null and void; in all moments."

"I release resonating or emanating with society; in all moments."

"I extract all of society from my beingness; in all moments."

"I extract all of society from my light emanation and sound frequency; in all moments."

"I shift my paradigm from society to the self-realization of my own empowerment; in all moments."

"I transcend society; in all moments."

"I am centered and empowered in the self-realization of my own empowerment; in all moments."

"I infuse the self realization of my own empowerment into my sound frequency; in all moments."

"I imbue the self-realization of my own empowerment into my light emanation; in all moments."

"I resonate and emanate the self-realization of my own empowerment; in all moments."

-Freedom Health Success-

The Reason You Aren't in a Relationship

Isn't it interesting that so many good and worthy people are without loving partners these days? Are we all flawed as we are conditioned to believe? Or, is the system flawed? I lost the need for a relationship when I fell in love with this guy from a dating service. I was so in love with him. I was gushing and happy. But he turned out to be a scam artist. He was not real.

The articulate writer passed me off to someone else to scam money from me. But what about these feelings? I felt love, incredible life-changing love, that made me happy and complete. But this guy wasn't real. It was then that I truly realized that the whole feeling of falling in love was generated by me.

I was in love without getting anything back from this guy. I was doing it. Then I realized if I was able to create the feeling of being in love unwittingly, then I could do it consciously as well. That was the last time I concerned myself with being in a relationship.

I also noticed that when great givers of life were suddenly in relationships, they turned their attention from their highest purpose to the target of their affections. There was always a dilution in their service to humanity in the some way. I see the relevance of so many aware souls who are uplifting humanity not being distracted in that way at this time.

Besides, we are expanded enough to be in love with all

life. We don't need to be placated by a linear relationship at this time. The love is always there. If you are feeling lonely, you are separating yourself with an outmoded concept that we are all separate. We are not. We are all living, being and creating in this incredible Love soup that is our mainstay now.

You are not alone. You may as well enjoy love in a billion intangible ways because it is our mainstay. That feeling that was tapped into--hit or miss--on some holidays, holy days, or with the company of one special person, is now your mainstay. It is just a matter of recognizing it, accepting it, and appreciating it.

When someone dynamic diverts their attention from their purpose to their beloved, their effectiveness is diluted. This is not how it was done in female energy. In female energy, there was an understanding that your partner was a key to awaken your own empowerment so that you have more to give to earth, Gaia and all beings. The way we have been trained to direct our focus onto the man is, in itself, a form of enslavement.

-Joy Love Abundance-

DO THESE FOR YOUR KIDS: Removing the Programming and Conditioning of Past Generations

In the last few hours, I have written and shared a few dynamic taps to help people get free of all their programming and conditioning. I spend my days exploring what they need to release so they will finally accept Joy, Love, Abundance, Freedom and Wholeness as a construct and a Universal reality. It seems that the more helpful a set of taps are, the more difficult they are to be seen by the people who do them.

It doesn't take everyone doing them. Look at the incredible shifts one person like Mandela or Gandhi made? It only possibly takes one person doing them as a surrogate for humanity for them to make a difference. Did you take note of how crazy last year was? It is because the taps are being done for humanity by incredible people like you.

Maybe you are the tipping point to bring about World Peace, perhaps, simply by doing these taps that I have been compelled to bring to you. The reason we are seeing so much negativity in the world is to prod us to accept our empowerment. Doing these taps is a simple way for everyone to do that.

Please don't tell me these taps are too long to do. Tell that to someone living in Aleppo.

(Say each statement three times out loud while tapping on

your head and say it a fourth time while tapping on your chest.)

“I declare myself a surrogate for my generation in doing these taps; in all moments.”

“I release being enslaved by the programming and conditioning of past generations; in all moments.”

“I release passing on the programming and conditioning of past generations to all generations; in all moments.”

“I remove all the programming and conditioning of past generations; in all moments.”

"I release using the programming and conditioning of past generations to validate myself; in all moments.”

"I release the genetic propensity to subscribe to the programming and conditioning of past generations; in all moments.”

"I release using the programming and conditioning of past generations to stay enslaved; in all moments.”

"I release using the programming and conditioning of past generations to feel safe; in all moments.”

"I release using the programming and conditioning of past generations to feel validated; in all moments.”

"I release using the programming and conditioning of past generations to feel empowered; in all moments.”

"I release using the programming and conditioning of past generations to enslave future generations; in all moments."

"I release being at the mercy of the programming and conditioning of past generations; in all moments."

"I release using the programming and conditioning of past generations to enslave future generations; in all moments."

"I release being used as a pawn to enslave all generations; in all moments."

"I release using the programming and conditioning of past generations to define myself; in all moments."

"I dry up all psychic streams that perpetuate the programming and conditioning of past generations; in all moments."

"I withdraw all my energy from the programming and conditioning of past generations; in all moments."

"I withdraw all my energy from the programming and conditioning of future generations; in all moments."

"I release being manipulated, coerced, duped, corrupted or enslaved by the programming and conditioning of past generations; in all moments."

"I remove all vivaxes between myself and the programming and conditioning of past generations; in all moments."

"I remove all tentacles between myself and the programming and conditioning of past generations; in all

moments."

"I remove all of the programming and conditioning of past generations; in all moments."

"I remove all of the engrams that all the programming and conditioning of past generations has put in me; in all moments."

"I collapse and dissolve all portals to the source of all programming and conditioning of all generations; in all moments."

"I release perpetuating the programming and conditioning of past generations; in all moments."

"I strip all illusion off of the programming and conditioning of past generations; in all moments."

"I remove all masks, walls and armor from the programming and conditioning of past generations; in all moments."

"I eliminate the first cause in regards to the programming and conditioning of past generations; in all moments."

"I remove all programming and conditioning that I have put on all generations; in all moments."

"I remove all engrams that I have put on all generations due to the programming and conditioning of past generations; in all moments."

"I remove all muscle memory of the programming and

conditioning of past generations; in all moments."

"I send all energy matrices into the light and sound that use the programming and conditioning of past generations to limit all generations; in all moments."

"I command all complex energy matrices that use the programming and conditioning of past generations to limit all generations to be escorted into the Light and Sound; in all moments."

"I send all energy matrices into the light and sound that perpetuate the programming and conditioning of all generations; in all moments."

"I command all complex energy matrices that perpetuate the programming and conditioning of all generations to be escorted into the Light and Sound; in all moments."

"I nullify all contracts with the programming and conditioning of past generations; in all moments."

"I nullify all contracts with all sources that perpetuates the programming and conditioning of past generations; in all moments."

"I recant all vows and agreements between myself and the programming and conditioning of past generations; in all moments."

"I collapse and dissolve all the programming and conditioning of past generations; in all moments."

"I remove all curses between myself and the programming and conditioning of past generations; in all moments."

“I remove all blessings between myself and the programming and conditioning of past generations; in all moments."

"I dissolve all karmic ties between myself and the programming and conditioning of past generations; in all moments."

"I cut all the cords and ties to the programming and conditioning of past generations; in all moments."

"I remove all the pain, burden, limitations, and controlling devices that the programming and conditioning of past generations has put on me; in all moments."

"I remove all the pain, burden, limitations, and controlling devices that I have put on all generations due to the programming and conditioning of past generations; in all moments."

"I take back all the joy, love, abundance, freedom, health, success, security, companionship, creativity, peace, life, wholeness, beauty, enthusiasm, contentment, spirituality, enlightenment, confidence, intellect, ability to discern and empowerment that the programming and conditioning of past generations has taken from me; in all moments."

"I give back to all generations all the joy, love, abundance, freedom, health, success, security, companionship, creativity, peace, life, wholeness, beauty, enthusiasm, contentment, spirituality, enlightenment, confidence, intellect, ability to discern and empowerment that I have taken from them due to the programming and conditioning of past generations; in all moments."

"I convert all the energy wasted from the programming and conditioning of all generations into exponential freedom for myself and all generations; in all moments."

"I release resonating with the programming and conditioning of past generations; in all moments."

"I release emanating with the programming and conditioning of past generations; in all moments."

"I extract all the limitations of the programming and conditioning of past generations from my sound frequency and the Universal sound frequency; in all moments."

"I extract all the limitations of the programming and conditioning of past generations from my light emanation and the Universal light emanation; in all moments."

"I shift my paradigm and the Universal paradigm from the programming and conditioning of past generations to exponential freedom for myself and all generations; in all moments."

"I, and all generations, transcend the programming and conditioning of past generations; in all moments."

"I am individually and universally centered and empowered in exponential freedom for myself and all generations; in all moments."

"I resonate, emanate and am interconnected with all generations in Universal exponential freedom for all generations; in all moments."

-Freedom Health Success-

Relationship Worksheet

The biggest issue that people seem to lament about is getting over a relationship with another person. That is because when you are intimate with someone, you swap energy freely. But when you part, you have left an energetic aspect of yourself with them. You walk around talking about them because you are trying to get your essence back from them. Here is the protocol to do just that.

Now you never have to suffer at the hands of a past lover and be left un-whole. Now you don't have to be hesitant to give all of yourself to the next person because now you have the means to energetically regain your empowerment. In fact, because these taps finish with "in all moments," you are safe guarded from being fragmented in the future as well.

This protocol is simply meant to put your fate back in your own hands where it should be. It is not merely words.

Doing this protocol is you being the shaman; it is you being empowered. It is you taking back your energy and releasing the things that have been weighing you down. It is also repairing your energy field so that you are not susceptible in the future. It is you taking back your empowerment and freeing you to love as unabashedly as you truly desire without the fear of being annihilated in the process.

It may feel so freeing to do these taps for past partners that you may want to do them regarding every person in your life. You may want to untangle yourself from every family member, co-worker, boss and friend. You may even want to do this protocol with every organization or idea that has held you back. Here is to you freeing yourself in a very profound way. Maybe in releasing all entanglements, you can finally get an understanding of who you really are unhindered and free.

You can make it a practice to do this once a day with a different person. You can even do it with groups, subjects, concepts and anything else that limits your freedom.

(Say each statement three times out loud while continuously tapping on the top of your head at the crown chakra, and say it a fourth time while tapping on your chest at the heart chakra.)

"I release being with ___________ out of habit; in all moments."

"I release feeling dependent on ____________; in all

moments."

"I release feeling beholden to ___________; in all moments."

"I release being enslaved to ___________; in all moments."

"I remove all vivaxes between myself and _____________; in all moments."

"I remove all tentacles between myself and _____________; in all moments."

"I remove the claws of ___________ from my beingness; in all moments."

"I remove all programming and conditioning that __________ has put on me; in all moments."

"I remove all engrams of __________ from my beingness; in all moments."

"I send all energy matrices into the Light and Sound that limit my freedom in regards to __________; in all moments."

"I command all complex energy matrices that limit my freedom in regards to __________ to be escorted into the Light and Sound by my Guides; in all moments."

"I strip all illusion off of my dynamics with __________; in all moments."

“I withdraw all my energy from ___________; in all moments.”

“I eliminate the first cause in regards to _______________; in all moments.”

“I remove all masks, walls and armor that I have worn because of ____________; in all moments.”

“I nullify all contracts with __________; in all moments.”

"I recant all vows and agreements between myself and __________; in all moments."

"I remove all curses between myself and __________; in all moments."

"I remove all blessings between myself and __________; in all moments."

"I sever all strings and cords between myself and __________; in all moments."

"I dissolve all karmic ties between myself and __________; in all moments."

"I remove all the pain, burden, limitations and engrams that _________ has put on me; in all moments."

"I remove all the pain, burden, limitations and engrams that I have put on ___________; in all moments."

"I take back all the joy, love, abundance, freedom, health, success, security, companionship, creativity, peace, life, wholeness, beauty, enthusiasm, contentment, spirituality, enlightenment and confidence that ____________ has taken from me; in all moments."

"I give back all that I have taken from ____________; in all moments."

"I release resonating with ______________; in all moments."

"I release emanating with ______________; in all moments."

"I remove all of _____________ from my sound frequency; in all moments."

"I remove all of _____________ from my light body; in all moments."

"I shift my paradigm from __________ to joy, love, abundance, freedom, health, success, security, companionship, creativity, peace, life, wholeness, beauty, enthusiasm, contentment, spirituality, enlightenment and confidence; in all moments."

"I strip all illusion off of ___________; in all moments."

"I transcend ____________; in all moments."

"I repair and fortify the Wei Chi on all my bodies; in all moments."

"I align all my bodies; in all moments."

"I am centered and empowered in joy, love, abundance, freedom, health, success, security, companionship, creativity, peace, life, wholeness, beauty, enthusiasm, contentment, spirituality, enlightenment and confidence; in all moments."

"I resonate, emanate and am interconnected with all life in joy, love, abundance, freedom, health, success, security, companionship, creativity, peace, life, wholeness, beauty, enthusiasm, contentment, spirituality, enlightenment and confidence; in all moments."

This opportunity to free yourself is my gift to you. The gift that you can give yourself is to recognize its value and to take this technique seriously. Devotion to a true love is noble. But many of us have spiritually outgrown blind loyalty. It is important for everyone's empowerment to know the difference.

It can also benefit you to give to your friends and family members who are dealing with a breakup. When they lament about another person, they are begging the Universe for help. This worksheet is the Universe answering their call through you.

-Joy Love Abundance

8: TRUTH

Answering a Concern from a Reader

Good morning! I'm sorry to bother you but I'm really feeling as though I'm being attacked from everywhere and everyone! I don't know what to think or where to start. Is it me? What am I doing wrong? I'm feeling really drained, sad and lost at this moment.

You are being attacked. I am as well. It is female energy that is being attacked and you are personifying it. It is not personal. And the attacks can't hurt you. They are shadows of what is trying to regain strength. They cannot. No need to feed them with fear. Just be glad that you are able to recognize the dynamics and understand that it is passing through like clouds crossing the sky.

-Freedom Health Success-

A Just Intention

The reason the world got so out of whack in the first place is because Female energy allowed male energy to do as it pleases. Female energy trusts and loves to a fault. Today is a chance for female energy to take back her empowerment. Male energy is expecting people to stand on the sidelines and allow it to do as it pleases once again. WE CANNOT AFFORD TO ALLOW THIS TO HAPPEN.

We, who love, love to a fault, and we must not confuse charity with compliance. The children of the earth are at stake. Female energy must go to that place she goes when nurturing those whom she loves. We must stand up for integrity, truth and justice. Bigotry, greed, war mongering and abuse of power must be abolished.

This is not the time to sit on the sidelines and comply. This is the time to stand centered and empowered in female energy, which is all permeating, all embracing and all empowered.

This is not a gender issue. It is embracing awareness and a just intention.

-Joy Love Abundance-

Another Perspective

Female energy doesn't do anything at all costs to win. That is male energy. Female energy is more interested in the betterment of all humanity through sharing its gifts. Female energy will step back if there is someone better to implement the uplifting of humanity.

Female energy is being empowered, not as an empty symbol, but as a strong unifying force that loves and empowers all, truly. There are so many beautiful examples of female energy on my page and in this world. They resonate with such a grace, integrity and beauty that having a woman who will do *anything* to succeed is an insult to their nature.

Yes, women are being empowered. More and more examples of female energy are emerging from the mist. But they emerge in truth and with the willingness to empower everyone along the way. We are now too savvy and have come too far to be fooled by a male figurehead cloaked in a thin veneer of femininity.

-Freedom Health Success-

The Dance of Empowerment

You have mastered the dance

In the swirl of earth's drama

Each step has been registered to memory

You have scraped and skinned your knees to the bone
Blackened and blued the ego beyond compare

You have convulsed in so much pain that your entrails
have repeatedly christened the ground

You have abased yourself to the point of curling up in a ball of regret and have forgotten how to unfurl

You have proved your worth again and again

Yet you are the one that craves evidence of your worth

You have nothing to prove

No wrongs to undo

Karma is no longer neatly allotted in weighed-out bags

Of punishment or forgiveness

All lines are blurred in a beautiful spectrum

Of give and take

Love and loss

Regret and forgiveness

Scorn and praise

We see our flaws in the reflection of the world's shortcomings

We can no longer cry victim or foul

For we realize that we hold the empowerment in our own cupped hands

Like a beautiful pearl of luminescent confidence

Not to clutch like a Louis Vuitton

But to blow like fairy dust in the face of humanity

A sheer mist of wonderment

To benefit all to awaken

To be satiated in expectation of true abundance and peace

You now realize to give sustenance is to symbiotically receive

To see Universal goodness emerge

Like sun rays through the cracks of a gray dawn

And pierce the hearts of the disgruntled

Warm the faces of the hopeful

Feed the souls of the downtrodden

Until all shift their dance from a monotonous two step

To a celebration of the exuberant

YOU DID THAT!

With the purity of your intention

The enthusiasm of your own quickened step

And your willingness to serve.

What Help Looks Like

You don't help anyone by feeling sorry for them.

You help them by seeing them as empowered and whole.

You don't help the world by talking about how hopeless you think it is and walking around shaking your head at all that is wrong with it.

You help the world by seeing it as beautiful, peaceful and clean. You hold that higher intention for the world. You are strong enough and self-disciplined to always see a higher expression of beauty and truth no matter what your outer senses experience.

You don't help yourself by listening to anyone else.

You empower yourself by delving into the depth of your own sacred well and seeing evidence of that sanctity in everyone you meet and the world around you.

Floodgates to More

Many people who have sessions with me and understand what I do are healer types. They may be inclined not to share what transpired, invite others to the group, or to have a session with me because they don't want to seem less effective to their own clientele. This is a male energy mentality and not worthy of female energy.

Sharing what I do will actually draw more people to that person because there are so very few people who are female energy in action. They will be magnets to the upgrade of female empowerment. Because that is what female empowerment does. Female empowerment gives everything it has and trusts that this never depletes it but simply allows it to be the floodgates to more.

This has been the heart-set that is my standard. I have had advisers lecture me on giving too much away so there is nothing proprietary about what I do. But that is having a very limited view of one's own empowerment. That is what male energy does. That is why we now have such a narrow band of truth to glean in society.

My Guides have been very emphatic. They have instructed me to pour out everything I possibly can into the mainstream of consciousness so it can't possibly be squelched by male energy trying to maintain domination. Such an intention affords exponential abundance and does not focus on monetary wealth, which pinches off all other forms of abundance. Male energy has done that to society as well.

Male energy has led humanity down a dead end street and nothing can free us except the exponential nature of female empowerment.

-Joy Love Abundance-

What Female Energy Does

The way female energy works is different than what male energy looks like. We are so trained to be goal oriented and view that as evidence of action. But sometimes the best action is inaction. Female energy right now is allowing male energy to spin its wheels and empty its tanks. That is why there is not a huge apparent shift in the world right now.

Think of how a wise, kind mother would do things. She would allow the other party to save face as much as possible and give them the opportunity to turn things around for themselves. This is what female energy is doing in the world right now. It is not about leveling the opposition. It is about coming to some kind of mutual respect and understanding.

A shift in dynamics in the world is not going to look like domination. That is male energy's way of expressing itself. A shift in dynamics is going to look like coming into agreement with a mutual respect. When you see this happening in the world, that will be evidence of the shift.

Right now, exclusively male-based structures are crumbling. When they patch themselves up with compromise and inclusiveness, that is evidence of a shift.

Female energy is about inclusiveness. It doesn't need credit or recognition. Male energy will prop itself up as victorious as long as possible. That is its way. We don't mind. We, who understand, take all things in stride. That is what female energy does.

-Freedom Health Success-

What Every Abuse Victim Knows

Believe it or not, a popular bully is performing a great service for all those who have been abused. What happens when someone is abused is no one believes them when they try to explain the personal vendetta they have been enduring. They are invalidated many times for their preposterous accusations.

So what a certain celebrity has been able to accomplish in displaying the abuser mentality is very helpful. He has been able to display and personify every faction of abuse that the victim has described but has usually been dismissed.

So seeing this behavior displayed openly is very validating to a victim. Next time someone describes the seemingly incredulous behavior of the aggressor, now all of society has an example to hold that person up next to. They can know for themselves that what the accuser is saying is possible. They will also get a sense of how vehemently and convincingly the abuser will refute it.

Such behavioral traits of the abuser are formula:

- Needing to be superior and protect their image
- Not taking any responsibility for their part
- Diminishing the victim
- Taking every situation personally
- Saying that the treatment was deserved
- Believing they were only defending themselves
- Believing that they are the innocent, they are the victim
- Twisting the scenario to seem credible
- Believing their own lies
- Truly believing that they are without fault.

The next time someone comes forward with an accusation that seems impossible because the accuser is such a great guy and an upstanding citizen, perhaps the authorities will think of someone they know who does this and take it more seriously. This is a great way to glean wisdom from the example that has been set before us. It is a great way to make lemonade out of lemons.

-Joy Love Abundance-

The New Dimension

What everyone needs to realize is that everything we were taught, even about healing, was a lie because it happened from the slant of a male dominated world. Anything that is centered in fear is still fear. There is no fear of taking on karma or of negativity when you expand into your female energy.

Love is the protective energy. Everything dissipates in the presence of love. There is no more fear. It is safe to be a healer and to speak truth now. We are in a new dimension now. We just have to relax and realize it.

-Freedom Health Success-

The Energetic Sex Talk

When you allow a man to shove his energy into you, you are left with whatever he gives because you have allowed him in. If he loves you, then he is pouring his love into you. But if he is not in love with you, he can shove any of his issues into you that he chooses. This is the recklessness of random sex.

The reason rape is so devastating and difficult to overcome is because a predator dumped his anger and hatred into the innocence of a victim. It is like mixing oil and water. She is left to deal with this energetic violation unless she is able to energetically remove his deposit. It is something that I assist with and there are taps that do this. I have shared them often.

Many times, a man is looking to let off steam or has issues around the practice of trolling for partners. He is not doing it out of the purity of his heart because he wants to gift women with his love.

If you are in a committed relationship and you have already agreed to support each other, then using sex to dissipate angst is a form of supporting each other. The angst is dissipated by the loving agreement involved. This truth is supported by the spiritual law of love which supersedes all other spiritual laws.

If you randomly use women to dump your issues into, then you are not going to be free of the issues. The issues may follow you around in the embodiment of the women you have used. Any man who is being stalked by a past lover may not realize that it is his issues in her compelled to get back to him.

It is your own issues that are stalking you. Your issues, in a sense, want to return to you.

The rule of thumb is, if there is no love for the other person, then the union is not sanctioned by spiritual law. Sexual engagement may lead to a karmic connection. Of course, we do meet people that we have loved in past lives and there is a passion in love at first sight. Maybe the sexual connection in those cases is getting together to return to each other all that you have held for them or taken from them in a past life. That may be all that is required.

-Joy Love Abundance-

The Difference Between Male Energy and Female Energy

Male energy says, "I have found the way! You must come to me to find it. Don't tell anyone. They cannot handle the truth. They must pay dearly for it. They must come through me because I found it. I am the one!"

Female energy says, "I have been presented with the way. It is marvelous what we are all capable of. Here, let me show everyone so that all can benefit. Please share with others so they can benefit as well. We are all empowered with this truth."

It is my purpose to balance the slate between male and female energy by sharing the truths that male energy has kept hidden from all but a chosen few all though modern history. This is what I do on my page and this is what we do in the group sessions.

Most people have been trained by male energy to feel helpless and that we have to suck up our fate. That is the great lie. We are empowered. We have always been. No group can withhold us from our state of Grace unless we give up ownership.

-Freedom Health Success-

Excerpt from a Group Call

"So, energetically there's this inner battle going on right now, and that's what my body's feeling. I make it so easy on the surface, but there's all these dynamics that go on energetically. And that feeling when a man diminishes you, or even when someone, even if you're a man...if someone with more clout diminishes you...that feeling you get in your body is what I'm dealing with right now, but I can't run away. I have to stay here and deal with it. And it's like that male energy...it's not [a person from group]; it's bigger than one person. He's being used as a surrogate, and if he would only realize that he's being used that way and it's okay, he would talk to me. So this is going on inwardly right now. You guys get a sense of it?"

"Yes," group responds.

"And I am not backing down. I am not backing down. I am not relinquishing this world to the bullshit of male energy. I am not.

"It feels like we're right up against the challenges that male and female energy--the dynamics--we're right up against that wall of pushing female energy into empowerment, and it plays out with us. My whole body is shaking right now, and I feel this wall in the third chakra. It feels like a cement slab in there, and it feels like it just shut down. And it doesn't feel like it's mine."

The group then did the following taps:

(Say each statement three times while tapping on your head and say it a fourth time while tapping on your chest.)

"We break down the wall or resistance; in all moments."

"We release the resistance of male energy to concede; in all moments."

"We release the resistance of female energy to empower herself; in all moments."

"We release the embedded roots of the ego; in all moments."

"We release the contempt for transcendence; in all moments."

"You know how many mind f#@ks I get all the time? Like, *This isn't important, you're not doing any good here, just forget about it, just stop worrying about it, you got your books out there, don't worry about helping anyone, who cares? Just go on with your life, figure out something else to do.*

"I mean it's constant. And without that flow, that

interaction, it's more difficult to maintain a center with this. I don't even feel confident that the message will get out there, sometimes. Sometimes, I rely on you guys telling me so because I don't know. I have a vision, but the mind f#@ks...they're not just mind f#@ks. They're whole energy f#@ks. They're sabotages on every level: physical, emotional, causal, mental...and sometimes they're all at once.

"And it takes ALL my energy just to hold space in a center and just to keep doing what I'm doing if I'm doing anything at all. No matter how whiney I sound on the surface, I hate sounding so whiney. It's like all the power plays in the world are hitting my body right now.

"I did not want to do this group session. I did not want to; I was dreading this call. But they have my back. You feel the Ancient Ones have my back? It's almost like they're propping me up for these hits, do you see that? (Tears...)

"Do you feel your own strength in here? What I do is not act in a group dynamic of a hierarchy; it should be random and fluid. Collecting people in a group net is not what it's about.

"But what's happening within these groups is I haven't been able...See, I haven't been handling things like you would see them handled by someone in a position of power. Because I don't deal in hierarchies or power, and that's why what we do here is not like anything you've ever known.

"What people would usually do is, when they're giving a critique, they would build up someone and tell them how valuable they are as a means to prepare them for what is to come... But that's not what I do, because that's not what I'm supposed to do. I'm supposed to take them by surprise, strip off the layers that cause their imbalances, and then leave them with that until they allow the layers to fall away. It's a whole different way than what male energy would do. Male energy would pacify them, patronize, really. I don't patronize. I mean even the word patronize is paternal, father, and now working with me we know what matronize does...(laughter).

"So bringing that up, that whole concept of marriage which men make this joke about resenting, was put in place by male energy. That's a perfect example of male energy being trapped in its own intentions. See, it's female energy, female energy is more indicative of not minding having lots of partners. Female energy can love anybody. It's male energy that usually can only love one person. So the whole concept of men going out and sleeping with a lot of women is them trying to do female energy because it's really women who are able to love that person they're with instantaneously.

"So the whole concept of marriage is meant for men to disrupt that fluidity in female energy that allows them to be able to love anybody. Male energy set up the confines of marriage, but then they curse female energy for what they've set up. It's hypocrisy. But what they, what male energy is maybe understanding right now, is there's more freedom in not needing to love just one person. And I'm not talking about married people. I'm just talking about in general out there. The whole hierarchy of controlling love so linearly, is slavery.

"Love is such a natural fluid expounding force. The way it has been squelched and limited in this world is ludicrous. It is bound to break out like a damn building up pressure. Not just within people but all of humanity. It needs to gush forth. We will see that in a renaissance of a creative source.

"Right now, there are the billionaires buying up any new technology that will advance us against freedom from fossil fuel. But soon, they will not be able to do that. They have their finger in the dam of linear existence trying to plug up progress. But that damn is bursting, and we are all witnessing as an old mentality dies and exponential freedom starts to burst forth.

"I mean we're touching on changing stagnant energy to the point of even breaking up the structure of marriage as it is in this world--that group dynamic of personal enslavement. And I'm not talking about on this call because you guys have spiritual agreements. That's much different than the controlling marriages that are out there that mock and scorn their partner. That contempt that you have for marriage is not about your relationship with your current mate, right? It has to do with the mass impingement on freedom and the systemic belief that if you are not in a committed relationship then you are damaged, unworthy or undesirable.

"I really appreciate you guys and thank you. Thank you for

your strength and understanding and endurance, I mean, um, you guys matter...you guys matter!"

-Joy Love Abundance-

Pro Truth and Awareness

The unborn is not a person. It is just a glob of cells with potential. Until it can think, breathe and exist outside of the body, there is no life in it. No two souls can operate the same space at the same time. It is Spiritual Law. When the baby kicks in the body, it is a knee jerk reaction like the snake moving after death. The soul that is intended for the fetus hovers around the body until inception.

Life begins at inception NOT conception. It is time for truth and understanding to prevail.

-Freedom Health Success-

Pro Love

The reason reincarnation is not openly accepted is because it directly challenges the importance of procreating. Endorsing large families is a form of control. Yet until the Dark Ages, reincarnation was written about in the Bible where Paul mentions being caught up in the third heaven. Purgatory, an on and off again teaching, is actually talking about reincarnating back to earth. I figured this out when I was four.

In the Dark Ages, the clergy were corrupt and would sell passageway into heaven. They took out all references of reincarnation from the Bible because it made their case stronger to sell passage into heaven. They realized that if people knew they would reincarnate, they would be less afraid and less willing to pay for preferential treatment. I learned this in a sixth grade social studies class.

Groups are energetic Ponzi schemes. They take in all the energy of the members and pool it out to those who need it as proof that the group is working for them. A group needs more and more energy to keep up the illusion of wealth. There are two ways to get more energy: by converting others or by creating more followers through having children. That is why the indoctrination of the next generation is important.

The rules must be strong and fear-based to keep people from going elsewhere. But the groups have reached a tipping point. There are less people left in the world to convert. So the main way to get more members is to have more children within the group.

Unless children are born within groups, those groups will eventually dwindle down to nothing. That may seem terrifying to some. That is the whole purpose of pushing for pro life. The groups are in survival mode and will do anything they can to survive, even use its members as pawns to keep its levels up. Not that this is done consciously, but energetically.

This truth needs to be said out loud. Those of us who know, know. The people who are taught that babies are being killed through abortion are being used as pawns to keep numbers high. They are creating a ground swelling of emotional drama that gridlocks the joy, love, abundance, freedom, quality of life and wholeness for all.

There is no shame in having an abortion. I am actually proud of myself for listening to my inner guidance that prevented me from bringing an unethical person into the world. Ever since I was a child, I wanted to have babies. So when I got pregnant by my first boyfriend, I was so happy. I was too young and insecure to realize what a truly selfish person he was. After we broke up, all his friends told me that he only seemed nice the time he was with me.

When I got pregnant, I was planning to have the baby out of the emotional desire to be a mother. I would have had to go on welfare and burden society with the cost of raising the child. I was fractured back then by all I had already endured in life. I would not have had the stamina to get out from under being a single mother. But I still was emotionally attached to having a baby. When a young person wants something, it is hard to get through to them.

But then my Spirit Guide, which was the only connection that was actually truth to me, showed me the Akashic records of the baby that would be born.

My boyfriend, the father, was a juvenile delinquent. He bragged how he set fires on trains and stole money from the elderly. I was shown how this baby was a karmic connection to the father, not me. The father needed the relationship with this baby and it would be like him. It would be selfish and manipulative and drain me of all resources leaving me depleted.

My boyfriend happily scheduled an abortion for me. When we went to the clinic, I was given a waiting room with another woman. She was from India, so she had the same point of view I did on the matter. I knew I wasn't killing anybody. Even in the Bible, it said that God made the body of man THEN breathed life into it. I also had been shown so many of my past lives that I knew that we lived regardless of the physical body. It was just an uncomfortable inconvenience.

The young Indian woman and I sat and chatted. We were not emotionally wrenched like in all the other rooms. I am not certain if this is true but she told me that in India, women who got pregnant by their husbands have abortions because they prefer to have babies by their lovers. She spoke of this as a by-product of arranged marriages. It was very funny to me. We were giggling and staff kept poking their heads in. We were the only room that wasn't energetically charged with gloom. The staff would stick their head in, and you could see them lighten

when they saw us engaging in light banter. Their heaviness lifted.

As soon as we got back to the apartment, with no regard for me, my boyfriend got on the phone to his two friends who had pregnant girlfriends and was telling them how easy it was. He was showing me how little he cared for me. Why did I not see that earlier? After more late night drug use and one broken rib over my heart, we separated. I am so grateful that my Spirit Guides got through to me when no one else could. I have regretted not having children in this life but never regretted not having that one.

Being the youngest of ten, I sometimes fantasized about being aborted. I resent that I was brought into such harsh living conditions when there was only contempt for me. My father got a lot of leverage and bragging rights out of having ten children. It was his only sense of accomplishment in this life. Both my parents were dynamic people whose ability to be great was squelched by the responsibility to keep us clothed and alive. Many nights we spent in the dark because the utilities were turned off. Many times we went hungry. Clothing and furniture were all other people's throwaways. I grew up feeling like a non-person.

I understand that there is a physiological transference that happens between the mother and the fetus. In a recent

Body Talk session, it was revealed that I was infused with such hatred at six weeks of conception because my mother resented the thought of another child. She had nightmares of being pregnant way before I came along.

I have always felt that anger for me. It is even more invalidating to be imbued with a resentment that can't be named. Being my mother's literal nightmare has affected my psyche this whole lifetime. Also, the lack of close nurturing has left me pretty devoid of intimate relationships. In my most private thoughts, I am grateful for the Spirit Guides, trees and nature for loving me when no human had it in them to love me. It is by divine intervention, my own perseverance and random kindnesses, that prevented me from going the route of a sociopath, I think. I am grateful to be over kind and loving and compelled to indulge in this extreme than the opposite.

But I still wonder what it would be like to be born to someone, anyone, wanting me.

-Joy Love Abundance-

Mary Magdalene was not a whore! Just saying.

-Freedom Health Success-

Subtle Energies

Your camera and binoculars both have a lens that needs to be adjusted to see within a certain range. They don't see everything. They just pick up the images within a certain range. Your cell phone has a signal that it picks up from a satellite tower to feed you the sound that you hear. So you have to be in range of a tower to get a signal for your call. You have to be in a certain range of people, so they can hear you unless you use a microphone and augment your voice.

These are all physical apparatuses that are subjected to time and space, meaning you have to be within a certain range of someone at the same time to connect with them. Or you need devices to augment the ability to perceive them. The human body is a physical apparatus as well.

The human body is hardware just like a camera is. It is subjected to the same limitations at the lens of a camera. This includes all its perceptions. Just like a camera, if the image is not in proximity, it will not get seen. It does not mean that it is not there. It means that the lens is unable to pick it up. That is what is happening with all our senses in regards to connecting with subtle energies. When someone crosses over, they don't really go anywhere. They take off the limitations of the physical body and then can perceive and be in a broader spectrum of life.

Linear understanding and perspectives do not serve us any longer. We are collectively shedding our skin to such things. The ridiculous notion that there is a beginning, middle and an end to life is quaint at best. But this concept has been used to enslave us to such a limiting reality. Most people don't know how to break free if they try. But try we must. This world of linear thoughts and petty competitions is choking the life out of humanity.

The good news is that the white knuckled grip of limitations is loosening its grip on us all. Humanity is taking its first gasp of awakening in what seems forever. Exponential existence will soon be our mainstay as all the old means of control are falling away. A way for this to happen is for everyone to get over themselves and realize that humans are not the most important form of life in existence. We feel that way because we are in the vantage point of the self and we have the ability to discern. Humans have used the ability to discern as a poisoned pen against all humanity by believing that they are the ruling party. That belief is the crosshairs where arrogance and ignorance intersect.

Humans use so many different ways to divide themselves into subsets of superiority: gender, race, religious or political affiliations, species, etc. They use this vantage point to diminish and desecrate all others who do not belong to their particular sect. They divide all of life into one huge pecking order with them as the superior being at the top. They spend all their existence competing for the highest position in this imaginary pageant of one-upmanship. They are fighting for supremacy in their own feeble realities and think that it is something that all of life subscribes to. But all of life is happily blending, flowing, merging and engaging all of life. It has not separated itself as people have so solidly done like spoiled cream at the top of a stagnant pool. That is what humanity has become. More and more people are sensing it.

The cure is to step willingly out of the position of superiority and regain an engagement with all of life. Many people are doing this with an appreciation of nature and a love for animals. They are experiencing such an awakening of inner connection between themselves and all of life. It is creating a resurgence of vitality within the lives of the individuals who are making an inner agreement to doing this. It is like they were in this stagnant eddy within a vibrant pool that was creating foam and scum from the lack of engagement with all life, and then they suddenly break free and join the fluid force of life again. These are indeed exciting times because of such a resurgence into the vibrant flux and flow of life.

There are ways to invigorate all of life with such a resurgence. It is quite simple in its purity and potential to churn the waters of life to a greater degree. It is done by simply acknowledging life in all forms and honoring all as equals. This includes every atom of life. This will be such a stretch for some people that they won't even be able to conceive of doing this. They are so hardwired into thinking that man is the most important being that they will not be able to stretch their imagination to such an extent. There are those who may be able to concede that humans are on the same level of importance as their dear pets, which are family members to them sometimes. That was rare in the past.

There will be those who will be able to stretch even further and get an understanding of the importance of trees and the world of foliage. They may be able to see them as an aspect of their environment that is necessary to sustain all of existence. It may be a stretch for them to feel that these forms of life are equal to them. But they may be able to stretch their capacity to get an understanding of their symbiotic relationship with trees outside the parameters of the mind. That may be the only way they can bring such a concept into balance. They may have to think of a tree as a sentient being by believing it has a human form in another reality. It may well have. But some may need to absolutely think this to quantify its value because they can't get there within the limitation of their own human arrogance that is hardwired in.

But there is another aspect of linear thought that few even consider as their equal. Ignoring it creates such a hard divide in the psyche of man that it needs to finally be addressed. It is the dividing line between animate and inanimate objects. Believe it or not, this form of discerning creates such a harsh separation between atoms of life that once this division is addressed and melted, all life will become fluid and regain a heightened sense of awareness. It will be raising the bar on what we all collectively accept and believe as life. It will evaporate that hard line between animate and inanimate and create a fluidity in life that has been missing up to this point in the evolution of human consciousness.

At one time, not very long ago, man felt that even their dear pets were not conscious beings and had no feelings or individual points of view. They thought of them as non-conscious and treated them as such. The more that man has been able to see the humanity in their pets, the more it has awakened a softness in themselves. This has resulted in a higher conscious awareness of their pets and themselves. It has awakened a greater capacity to love.

Pets are now seen as loving companions and worthy of compassion and care. The evolution in our pet's treatment has created a more fluid understanding of animals in general. It has created a bridge for us to realize that all animals are capable of love and other qualities once thought only human attributes.

It has heightened our awareness of their capabilities and has heightened our compassion for them. It has heightened our awareness in general. In many cases, pets and animals came to matter as much or more than human family members.

At first, this was just an individual thing. But more and more, people could see how important other people's pets were to them. There is now more of a universal understanding of how our love connection with our family of animals is very important to our quality of our life. More and more people are realizing that life is less enjoyable without the connection to their furry, scaly, or feathered companions. We have an aversion to seeing them harmed. Our pets and the wild critters that visit us in our yards have become a vital part of our enjoyment of life. It is a means to reconnect to that aspect of ourselves that we have shut ourselves off from. We have started to realize our existence as an aspect of nature. In a sanitized way, it has allowed us to emerge back into nature through our love for animals. This, in itself, has had a drastic effect of softening the edges of the humans with this awareness.

This connection with our pets has awakened an incredible byproduct of compassion and caring in us that has bled over into the mainstay of life. The love is spilling over into all our interactions. Those who love their pets have a softening of their energetic skin. They are no longer in brute mode where they believe life is all about them. They honor life in other forms because the blind spots where they are not able to reach an understanding with other humans are blurred when there is an animal involved. It is so much easier for some to let down their guard with an animal because they realize that an animal is not judging them. Dogs, cats, birds, or fish do not deem us as unworthy. They do not dissect us in a multitude of subsets like intelligence, economic status or attractiveness level. The animals and the animal kingdom have one classifying discernment: Are they safe to trust or not?

Because they are not being judged by an animal, they don't recoil and harden their energetic edges to defend themselves. They happily send their energy out in all directions around the animal because it is their innate nature to do so as well. It has been difficult for man to be so contained in the sarcophagus of his own stagnant pool of energy. So now given the opportunity via the appreciation of non-judging beings, he is able to send his energy out in a way that he has not allowed himself to up to this point. It has created a more fluid way of interacting with others. Because once someone gets used to being able to relax the edges of their energy, they want to do it more and more. It is like loosening your pants and being comfortable. In society, it used to be a necessity to dress in starched and uncomfortable garbs. This was a reflection of the limiting range of the consciousness of the time. But as man loosened his garb, so has he loosened his stance in regards to his true engagement of others. Up until now, the consciousness of man has been as tightly starched as his Sunday collars. But now, we are unbuttoning our energy fields and more able to loosen our belts with our interactions with others.

There is another pushing of the envelope in our understanding of life as more and more people embrace the wisdom of trees and see them as the beings of intelligence that they are. In the near future, there is going to be such a sense of shame as to how humans have treated trees in the history of the planet. There is vital wisdom lost every time one of these sentient beings is destroyed. The Sequoias and the Redwoods should be preserved and honored because of the history of the planet they hold. They speak this wisdom to all who will listen. Perhaps they hold wisdom for this planet as ignorance has become systemically encouraged as a form of control upon the masses. But to power's chagrin, humans are taking an evolutionary jump that it has been unable to thwart.

Man is evolving to the point that many will able to soon easily communicate with trees. It is already happening. As this understanding unfolds and communication commences, man will get a greater awakening of truth than ever before. The most ignorant statement that Ronald Reagan made while he was in office is, "If you have seen one Redwood, you have seen them all." This shows the depth of ignorance that was prevalent at the time. Those who admire this man are showing the lack of awareness or the programming that was once our mainstay. The more this statement is readily seen as ignorance, the more it is a gauge for the awakening of the planet.

People know that trees and plants provide oxygen in exchange for carbon dioxide. They take our waste and recycle it back into purity for us. But what people have yet to realize is that trees and foliage extract our angst, worry and hate, absorb it like fertilizer, and replace it with love. This is what they have been doing for us all through existence. They have been the silent watchers to our worries and troubles. They have nurtured us when we did not even realize that they were aware. So many people who want to know who their spirit guides are, they lack the awareness or capacity to realize that their spirit guides are sometimes planted in their own back yard. The more that people start honoring trees, the less insanity there will be in the world. In fact, troubled communities and violent parts of the world could be spontaneously shifted back into balance, by planting many trees in them.

The parts of the world where there is more infighting and crime are the parts in the world where there are fewer trees. If these areas could be automatically implanted with trees, we would see the hostility rate, infighting and mental illness frantically dissipate. Maybe even perhaps even the dis-ease that we are presently seeing. As miraculous as the known benefits of trees are in supplying our oxygen, it's amazing that they are valued as little as they are. That is evidence of a disconnection between humans and all other life forms of life caused by man's insistence that they are the superior race. It is with a sweet interest that trees look onto the humans who think they run the planet. The real thing that they do is run the planet to the ground. The trees look down on us with the similarity of loving acceptance of a parent whose five year old believes that they are grown and in charge. That is how they perceive us.

It is an interesting fact that trees enjoy the company of their humans on the planet. It may be thought that they would prefer to be in a forest with all of their own kind. This is not the case. They enjoy watching the interactions of their humans and think of themselves as family members in our lives. They watch over us and have energetic influence in protecting us from unnecessary harm. They are able to reassure one of such protection if one has the ability to ask for it. Many times, they protect their humans without even being asked. They can create an energetic force field around the home of their people.

When I moved into my new home, I was uncomfortable my first night in a strange house. I had that feeling of vulnerability in being in a different setting. It was one of the very old trees in the front yard that reassured me that nothing was going to happen to me in my home. That he was able to maintain protection around my home afforded me the luxury of safety. There is an incredible feeling of being valued on my new property, like I was handpicked to be guardian of a subtle gateway between man and nature. It has become so as the backyard is brimming with wildlife creatures that I never thought I would be so honored to observe so closely.

One would think that this is just something that I may be conjuring up within myself and projecting onto the tree. This may be the case if it weren't for the fact that the trees do not appease me and tell me what I want to hear. They have a unique and distinct point of view that is prevalent the more one learns to listen. This was evident when I was listening to the neighbor boys playing and screaming as children do. It was an annoyance to me. But the same wise old tree distinctly chimed in to my mental banter and mildly chided me. He showed me how much the trees enjoyed watching these boys play and grow. It brought them such pleasure that they did not want that hindered in any way. It was their way of protecting the boys from me as well. Then they showed me how the boys needed to scream and carry on as part of their tools to maintain balance. The screaming was their way of dissipating stagnant energy similar to what I do in a private session.

The trees do enjoy people and they think of themselves as family members. They do not divide themselves into little parcels the way that humans do with their property lines. So they don't comprehend why the humans on the other side of the street never acknowledge or engage them. These boundary rules that humans quantify everything with are so silly that it is hard for them to fathom. They are immersed in all of life all over the world. Then they watch the humans create these invisible dividing lines between themselves and all others. It is ridiculous to them. The other thing they find very nonsensical is how man will display such determination to cut down a huge patch of trees only to plant more trees in straight little rows. They are fascinated by the lengths that men will go to do this. Yes, men. Women are not so interested in making trees be diminished in this way. They just see it as man's displaced need to control all aspects of life to compensate for his insecurity in not sincerely feeling empowered.

I learned about tree's great pastime of watching their humans grow when I taught a woman to communicate with trees. She found herself in her neighborhood that she grew up in. She sat with a tree that she used to pass when going to the grocery store. As she sat next to the tree in her car, her tears filled with joy at the communion she was experiencing. What this tree conveyed to her was that he remembered her as a child. He was able to help her tap into the pleasant memories she had forgotten. She remembered, with the tree's assistance, the simplistic joy of playing. Then he went on and told her more.

He told her how he so missed watching the children play under his branches. It wasn't until later that she realized there used to be a small playground that the tree overlooked. Watching the children play brought the tree much pleasure. Realizing this and coming to this awareness with her own connection with the tree brought such a life-changing awakening to this woman. She was changed forever. When people go back to a neighborhood where they once lived and get a warm welcoming feeling, many times it is the trees remembering them and happy to see them. Although they may never acknowledge the trees, the trees acknowledge them and send them such love. To the trees, it is like getting a visit from a grown child that long ago went off to college and never returned.

There is a pleasant stretch of road I drive where the trees line the path on each side. It makes me happy just to ride down that road. I was made aware that I was benefiting from the trees' natural happiness they exude. I communicated with them one day and they showed me their amusement of watching the people in the car have one mindset in the morning and change to a frantic demeanor when they returned at night to their little home boxes. They showed me how they had their favorite people. Some were mean to their children and they would send love to the babies in the back seats and calm down the humans who were being mean or angry to their children.

The row of trees worked collectively to shift the mood of the people as they drove by so that they would be kinder. It was very easy for them to take the people's angst. That is why it was such a pleasant stretch of road to travel. The trees were consciously working together to smooth out the issues of all those who traveled on that road. Perhaps they felt my ability to appreciate them and chose to talk to me just then. Perhaps they avail themselves to speak to all who will listen. I suspect the latter. It would be such a more expansive world if more people seized the opportunity to speak to these wise souls while they have the opportunity to do so.

I created a page on social media called the "Wisdom of the Trees" because the trees want to communicate with humans. They want to help them become more aware. The trees told me that they communicate with all life similarly to how we communicate on social media. But since we didn't have this understanding of social media until very recently, we couldn't have fathomed this sooner. Without social media, we would never have been able to understand how trees are able to connect with other trees on the other side of the world. Now that we do this, we can appreciate more fully how they are able to know so much beyond their own swatch of earth. The trees wanted a way to socially interface with humans and had me set up a page where they could do this. It is called, "The Wisdom of the Trees" because that is what it is. But humans have not been able to quite grasp the incredible opportunity this was to learn from treekind. I have been remiss in explaining it well. So it has become mostly a page that posts pretty pictures of tree. It is a shame because trees have so much truth to share.

I learned a lot about trees when I started a little forest of seedlings while living in my last apartment. I have four hundred saplings living in pots on my back balcony. Of course, man had to get involved in sabotaging my project by complaining they were interfering with using the balcony as a fire escape (which they were not). I ended up bringing them inside for the winter as the complex needed to repair my balcony. I would water them every day and was amazed at how much love and warmth they exuded. I learned that they had distinct preferences as well.

The baby saplings enjoyed it when I would sing to them or play music for them. They seemed to like some of my contemporary music but also enjoyed classical music. They enjoyed Mozart the best and were less enthused about Beethoven. The way I knew is that I would get this opening energy within myself when they liked something and this tightening energy within when they didn't like something. It was very subtle because they don't have desperate needs and desires like humans do. It was just more like a mild preference. But they had these sweet little points of view and it was amusing to be inundated by so many polite individuals all at once.

They were always sweet and loving with me as they understood my intentions with them. They showed me times in the past when trees went out of their way to assist me because of my future validation of them. There were many little cherry trees in my sapling forest. They showed me a time I remembered when I was hungry as a child. They reminded me of this one corner lot where cherry trees went into bloom specifically to provide a plethora of cherries as a means of feeding me and loving on me. They were gifting me in advance for my love and connection to them. Trees and animals are not so trapped in time and space and this was an example of that. They knew all that I was in my infancy. I felt ashamed because my siblings and I would break off braches to pick all the cherries that we couldn't reach up to get. The trees reassured me that they understood my undeveloped mentality then and were still happy to oblige me. They showed me a kindness and a tolerance that no human had shown me. Trees all over the world do this for so many people. I bet looking back now, you can see how the trees were validating and supporting you. Sometimes when I thought I was talking to God, a tree was answering.

There was a time though that I chided my cat Smudge for climbing amongst the saplings and chewing off their leaves. They chided me in return for interfering with their relationship with Smudge. Smudge was a dear friend and they did not want me to come between them and him. I understood immediately and never ran interference again. There was a time recently when I had a vase full of flowers defend Smudge in a similar way. They were on the table and Smudge was chewing into them and knocked them over. I yelled at Smudge. When I took the flowers to the sink to fill their water, I heard these sweet little strains in an energetic chorus of distinct personalities, coming to the defense of Smudge. They were not saying this in words, but I heard loud and clear in tiny little voices, "Don't yell at Smudge. He is our friend."

The relationship people have with animals and plant life is one of friendship. They are not hindered by the linear protocol that humans are superior. Animals and plants are friends and there is no superiority involved. Years ago, while walking my dog, he peed on this very small lilac bush. I tried to stop him because I didn't want the urine to kill the tree. The tree came forth to let me know that he appreciated the camaraderie with my dog and did not want him to stop peeing on him. It was an important relationship for him that he looked forward to. The urine didn't bother him but the lack of connection would have.

Where people ignore trees so often, dogs pay them homage. They sniff at the bark of a tree similarly as they will the leg of a human. Dogs do not discriminate.

Another way I experienced camaraderie between different species was when I put a plant and some snails into my betta fish's bowl. To him, they weren't decoration. They were friends and company. They were a reminder of life outside the bowl. I realized that while a fish is physically in the bowl, most of his essence is in the ocean. But seeing the relationship between the fish and the plants in the bowl was another way I realized the symbiotic relationship between plant life and other species. Humans have it too, but they aren't so readily aware of its importance. I also learned that other species have an ability to discern and have preferences. I learned this when I added a particularly large snail to the fish's bowl. He did not like it. They did not get along for some reason. He felt like this snail was an intruder in his home. He had not minded other snails. But this one he did not like. It was very subtle, but I felt a distinct dislike between them. They learned to coexist but it was an adjustment for the fish.

Now that many of us can accept and appreciate the consciousness of animals, and more and more are recognizing consciousness in plants and trees, there is another quantum leap of understanding that needs to be taken. It is time for the acknowledgement and wisdom of the life force and consciousness in inanimate objects. Some people are already there. They have a fondness for rocks and understand the inherent wisdom in them. They connect with precious stones on a very deep level. They feel the benevolence of their assistance in adding to our quality of life. You hear this when people say rocks are very special to them. But the life force in inanimate objects runs much deeper than merely in the rocks and precious stones that we gravitate to. There is consciousness in all inanimate objects.

Atoms are the building block of all things--inanimate and animate alike. There is consciousness in every single atom regardless of whether it is inanimate or animate. Since all the atoms that come together to form any item are alive, it only goes to reason that the group that they form is a life form as well. The atoms that come together to form any object do so in agreement with the other atoms of the grouping. This agreement forms a group consciousness of living atoms and, in itself, is considered a form of life even though it doesn't move or express itself in the course senses that we use to define life. It is expressing itself in the more subtle perceptions that are less tangible than the others. But they are indeed expressing their nature in subtle ways as living, validated beings.

You can say that they don't matter because they don't express emotions like love. But love, in the ways humans express it, is merely love being pumped through a glandular system. The fact that inanimate objects don't do that may not be their weakness. It may be our weakness in the need to express love through our physicality. Perhaps inanimate objects are more pure in their expression because they have no need for outer validation to define the parameters of who and what they are. It is humans that vacillate between their omnipotence and the lack of any self-awareness or esteem whatsoever. In fact, tapping into the stillness of inanimate objects may be a means of getting in touch with our own stillness. Perhaps that is what we fear as fragile humans: being so expansive that we don't recognize ourselves beyond self-induced limitations.

Humans aren't afraid to die usually. Humans are afraid to be separated from their consciousness. They fear the expansiveness of awareness that makes them believe that they will not be a contained entity when they transcend this world. They are afraid of their omniscience because it implies that their atoms will be poured into a collective group, and they will have little identification with self. This is a limited belief system. We will always have our vantage point of self even when we transcend self. It isn't a matter of giving something up to transcend. It is a matter of adding exponentially to our repertoire of self. We are no longer one vantage point. We can be fluidly in agreement with any and every vantage point at once while still maintaining our identification with self. Believing otherwise is merely a trap to prevent humans from experiencing the awareness and empowerment that they are capable of.

Children have an innate understanding of the expansiveness of life and how inanimate objects have consciousness. Just watch the relationship they have with their toys, teddy bear or doll, and you will get a sense that these items are real to them. They have profound relationships with them. When they lose a favorite item, there is a real sense of loss. We dismiss these experiences and wait for them to outgrow such things. We may even prompt the outgrowing of these relationships along by dismissing them. This may be doing our children and ourselves a disservice. Perhaps the way that adults separate the world into real and imaginary or alive and inanimate, is one of the great forms of disservice that we as a species do to ourselves. Perhaps we would be better served in leaving the wonder in life. A means to doing this is in accepting the sanctity of inanimate life forms, alongside those living beings.

There is a passage in the Bible that says something to the effect of becoming like the little children to see the kingdom of God. The way to do this is by tapping into the sweetness and sanctity of non-animated life and treating it with the respect that you would a living being because the essences are made up of the same element. By doing this, you will be able to not only delve into the wonderment of the childlike realms, you will also be able to tap into the stillness that inanimate life avails. Perhaps the only way to truly embrace your deepest stillness is by honoring life in all forms without a hint of judgment or need for quantification. This includes inanimate life. Perhaps this is the formula of enlightenment and the reason that so many have a difficult time breeching the doorway of transcendence. Perhaps, it is not met by walking through doors but having the agreement to walk through walls via the inanimate world.

Perhaps inanimate objects and what we call living beings is the last divide of judgment and arrogance. Perhaps if one is able to accept the realms of the inanimate beings as valid, they can gain passage through all of life. Perhaps it is a formula procedure of mixing the realms of the living with the stillness and wisdom of the inanimate beings. Perhaps blurring the lines between the inanimate and animate creates the whole of awareness that so many truth seekers are seeking. It may be easy to dismiss. But for those open to love in all forms, surely they can stretch their capacity to see beyond what the glandular system can process as love. Perhaps inanimate objects are overlooked because of their inability to stroke the ego of humans no matter how well they serve. Perhaps humans overriding this need can be very beneficial in stretching their capacity to love. Love is only warm and fuzzy when it strikes a chord within the emotions. But love, in its pure unadulterated form, is more of a nothingness and a peace that is let un-agitated by petty emotions. Perhaps reaching this state is a secret held in the realms of that inanimate world.

A great technique to develop an appreciation for inanimate objects is to start to see them as an embodiment of a group of live atoms that have come together to serve a purpose. See them just as valid as the human body or the body of a beloved pet. Perhaps such items around our home are deemed inanimate because of our lack of acknowledgement of them. Perhaps if we started to appreciate them and validate them, there would be an awakening of a mutual respect between us and them. Are artificial flowers any less valid to bring beauty to a room? Is a vacuum cleaner not the most important entity when you need your rug vacuumed? These are the things to consider. These simple acknowledgments of gratitude do not need to be demonstrative. Perhaps this technique is a shortcut to developing the reverence that holy men have sought through history. Perhaps this is the upgrade in the practices of a truth seeker searching for understanding.

A great way to tap into this reverence is to adopt an inanimate being like a plush animal or doll as a dear companion. See its personality come through, and honor it like a child would do. Develop a relationship with that object that is intimate and sincere. Use this item to pour all your love and gratitude into the inanimate realms. The gratitude opens portals that nothing else will. These portals into inanimate realms may be a means to self-awakening. This can also be done with your tools, car, musical instrument or a variety of other items as well. But there is something magical in crossing the boundaries of what is acceptable as an adult and stepping back into the childlike wonderment that we are pushed out of all too soon.

By taking a leap of understanding and consciously committing to disregard the rational mind of adulthood, you will be blending the two worlds of reality and imagination. They will meld into a splendid array of whimsical intrigue. This is a precursor to existing consciously in the enlightened worlds. Use an inanimate plush toy as a portal to pour all your love and sincerity into the inanimate realms. It will be a means to capture all the elixir of your precious intentions without allowing one drop to go into the hands of ignoble causes. Allow your children to do the same as long as they are capable.

Children's unadulterated intention and innocence is a powerful force in awakening the mass consciousness of this world. It has never been the caretaker's job to pull their children into the harsh worlds of this reality. It has always been the loving parents' job to allow their children to stay free of the fray of mental inundations of a harsh reality as much as possible. This changed when parents started using their children to compensate for their own lack and wound them up like little competitive machines to please themselves. It is time to give our children back to love and allow them to be sensitive, kind, imaginative, different and quirky as much as they choose to be. The more expressive and creative a new crop of children are, the more enlightened and empowered we all become in the awakening of a new dawn.

It is like most people use inanimate objects as a backdrop for their life. They are creating a schism that we in human form have become accustomed to. But by accepting the inanimate world into your fold, it is like you are pulling that backdrop off the wall and wrapping it around you to enhance the wonder of all your experiences. By doing this, you will be able to read children books with new insights and new awareness. For a byproduct of such intentions is to unlock the iron vault of your own subtle perceptions. It is to give the main driver of your own visualization and manifestation powers wings. You will be able to go into the realms of the imagination first as a guest and then as a licensed citizen. These energies that lie flat and immobile around you will start to come to life and engage you in a very valid way.

If we were still in the third dimension, suggesting this would seem insane because anyone so free of the limitations of the mind would be judged as insane. But with all the insanity and depravation that we are all witnessing in the world, insanity is the current mainstay. Nothing makes sense or has any accord in the way things are presently run or managed. These are the walls that must give way to higher empowerment. Living devoid of acknowledging inanimate objects as life is like putting all your weight in one half of a ship and expecting the ship to be balanced. We are living half an experience right now by not acknowledging inanimate items as life. We have been run to the ground with such imbalances, and it is time to reclaim the whole ship.

Did you know that trees are not lifeless beings but they undulate like flora under water? Most people can't see this movement because the lens of their vision and the wiring of their brain make them believe that trees are still. But by me telling you how I see a tree move, others will start to experience this reality. Then at a point, everyone will be able to see trees undulate. Then the era that we thought trees were non-moving will be a thing of the past. This is also true with non-linear existence. When people stop mindlessly accepting the limitation of linear time and limited space, all of humanity will move to expressing itself in more freeing realms. We will all be experiencing in exponential increments that are not yet collectively defined.

It will happen as more and more drop the limitations of being mind-centered and move to being heart-centered. The world was duped into believing that the mind was the highest achievable attainment in the quest for omniscience. This is a trap set up by the mind to assure its continuation.

Children are naturally heart-centered. Then they are scolded, bullied, manipulated and lied into becoming mind centered. Those who are not able to give up such sweetness are labeled flaky, weak, oversensitive or mentally unbalanced. Those who try very hard to transition to mind-centered become depressed and even suicidal. The pain of foregoing such sweetness becomes unbearable.

When our young people are sent off to war and experience such atrocities and sacrifice their limbs, they return only wishing to be of the heart again. When this happens, the world, which has been conditioned to worship the mind, turns on them. There is no place for people of the heart in such a world. They become homeless or end up on permanent disability. They are still better to have returned to the heart. But it is such a harsh means of getting them there.

Enlightenment happens through dropping the limitations of the mind and going forward into realms that a mind can't fathom. It is like trying to convince someone who has no connection to nature about the beauty and reverence that is found in immersing oneself in the experience. They will only get agitated because their mind will pull them away from being drawn to such things. It is no matter. Those of us who come from the heart have the patience and tolerance to awaken people's hearts without ever disturbing their minds. When their heart is opened to such an extent that the control of others through mind reason and manipulation no longer appeals to them, they will easily open up to love like energetic blossoms.

This is how we have done it and this is how it has always been done in the realms of energy. That is why the analogy of a flower blooming is so profound. It depicts the individual going from seeing himself as a linear being (a stem and a bud) and expounding forth into an energetic bloom. This is what our love avails each being. This is why our unconditional love is so profound. It is a means of encouraging each soul to burst forth into awakening. This is the least of what we do now in the shift that is happening in these realms. This is what we came here for, to experience the mass blossoming of a new era.

You are a part of this in wondrous ways that have never before been articulated. Yet you instinctively know this as your truth. Embrace your wonderment. Immerse yourself in the excitement that the inanimate world has to offer. It is one of being acknowledged and beckoned to join the dance of life. Do this in your own life as a means to quicken the pace of our expansion. It is a new era, a new dawn, and a new awakening as all life mixes, expands and rolls into itself to complete the alchemy of enlightenment. You matter. As all souls do and all collection of souls do. Enjoy the expansion of this awareness and know you are expounding into love and are more a part of life than ever. It is not possible to be separated from your consciousness because you are the consciousness and heartbeat of love, as we all are.

There is no longer a need to fight and scrap in a competition for love. You know who you are now. You are awakened and fixated in the perfect fluidity of life.

As deeply as I am capable of loving, you are loved, and more.

Joy Love Abundance-

Let the Truth Be Known

Say each statement three times while tapping on your head and say it a fourth time while tapping on your chest.

"The path to Truth is cleared; in all moments."

"All obstacles to Truth are dismantled; in all moments."

"The pathway to Truth is exponentially widened; in all moments."

"All those who oppose Truth are awakened; in all moments."

"Truth is the mainstay; in all moments."

"All associating male energy as bullies is removed; in all moments."

"All abusive energy is removed from male energy; in all moments."

"All superiority is removed from male energy; in all moments."

How to Tell If You Are Still Coming from Male Energy

Many times I post the most profound taps that will be very beneficial to everyone. But they go undone by so many. The statements I hear are that they don't seem relevant to them, so the people don't the taps. That is coming from male energy still.

Here is the thing. We can no longer benefit from something on the backs of others. If we are going to succeed as individuals, it is going to be with the intention for everyone else to succeed as well. That is what the new paradigm entails.

There is no longer win at all costs, dog-eat-dog, going behind someone's back, kill or be killed. These are all outmoded, linear concepts. The way to thrive in the new paradigm is to ensure that everyone thrives as well. We are all becoming empaths, so we can feel each other's pain.

From experience, I can tell you it is more excruciating to feel the pain that passes through others than to feel your own. To take it further, no pain is original to us. That has been the lie. We have always carried it for others and then manifested it in our own experiences. Now is the time to be more aware of what we have always been doing. The one example that comes close is experiencing the discomfort of your child. This is what we have been doing with everyone else yet once or twice removed. Now is the time to be more conscious.

So when I put out taps that benefit all of humanity, they are the most expedient way to assist ourselves. If you want to jump into the new paradigm, operate from the mentality or "heart-ality" of helping others. You will notice a clear benefit and shift much more quickly than if you are still operating from an egocentric perspective.

-Joy Love Abundance-

Hot Flashes

A friend asked me about hot flashes. She has been going through them for years. She was wondering why she hasn't passed through that right of passage more quickly. Nothing the doctors give her and none of the natural remedies have worked for her.

This is what came through to tell her: “You are agreeing to it. You have heard all these stories about menopause and how horrible the symptoms are and you have agreed to every one of them for yourself.”

There is a shift that happens during this lifecycle. Women exist in this male-based society that exists on a foundation of lies. Lies that men are superior, lies that women are here to serve men, lies that unequivocally treat women as inferior species, lies that treat other life forms as inferior, lies that treat the earth like its own private wrecking site. This is all contra to how female energy honors the connectedness of life.

When women get older, they tap into their wisdom. They are no longer ruled by their urges to love, serve and have babies. They are tapped into their truth. It is so counter to what they have been putting up with that it causes a physical reaction in the body. It is similar to the way a body reacts when it has had powerful healing work done. But because women still belong to a society that sees them as inferior, their shift into wisdom is seen as an affliction. It is an inconvenience to a male dominated society. They want women issues to be dealt with in a way that doesn't interfere with their game, something they can compartmentalize. So they treat it like an illness.

Female energy has stepped so far away from her truth, that as a group, it has accepted the shift in her life cycle as an inconvenience and a problem if not an illness. If she were more able to fully grasp the totality of her own empowerment, she would allow the shift to happen and to even embrace it so that it happened quickly and easily.

Now back to my friend's hot flashes. I led her through taps about being burned alive. These so resonated with her. She felt that she had been burned as a witch in a past life. So many of us have. It is the reason she does not give more voice to her truth and is afraid of her second sight. In fact, she did that tap, "I release the fear of my second sight; in all moments."

The reason she was having continued hot flashes was that she was dealing with the trauma of being burned alive. But since she wasn't allowing herself to embrace the truth of that experience, it was taking many years for her to shift into her truth. The reason she denied herself truth in this lifetime was because she was burned alive for her truth in a past lifetime. The residual effects were her being trapped in the feeling of burning up in this lifetime. Getting closer to her truth in this lifetime was the trigger for the hot flashes. Anger was the frustration of realizing there was a better way to deal with the situation and not having the skills to release the frustration of being burned alive as it took over the present physical body.

I led her through more taps, which helped her stop treating menopause like this great illness, and instead celebrate it as a rite of passage to advance more into her truth. We will see how it works for her. This truth in itself may work to help others as well.

-Freedom Health Success-

Fiction or Non? For the Love of Goddess

When I was imprisoned, I was privy to the psychic imagery of my captor. It was real to me. He had done much research on conspiracy theories and when I tuned in, I could tell him information that he felt was as accurate as anything he had researched but also filled in a lot of gaps for him. I became his muse for anything regarding the other races and planets in the galaxy.

I got very detailed images of other planets. There was one that was really bad. It scared me. It actually created voracious jealousy in me even though I am not a jealous person. In a very vivid experience, in a past time, they drugged my captor and me and took us to their home planet and sold us. We were sold into slavery to be turned into human cyborgs to be soldiers in a galactic war. I watched as they performed the surgery on my captor and harvested his brain. I stuttered a week after that experience.

We called the planet that acted as slave traders "the cat people planet." They were humanoid and looked like sultry exotic women. They were manipulative, cunning, ruthless and heartless. They operated devoid of compassion. They had the ability of trapping men with their exotic, lithe beauty. I see traces of them in some female women. Some women who make themselves up like beautiful war paint and wear the stilettos makes me think that the "cat people" are an archetype that women are trying to live up to. Also, I wonder if people who hate cats are really reacting to the cat people.

I have never told anyone about this because it sounds crazy, and the experience with my captor was maddening. But recently, when I facilitated a session with a long time client, and she was still having panic attacks, we did taps on releasing her relationship with the cat people. They resonated with her and she had a strong reaction in doing them.

I was contemplating why earth has been male oriented for all of modern history and why it has demonized women so thoroughly. The answer that came was that the cat people, at one time in history, preyed upon earth men. It was such a horrific and helpless experience that they developed an aversion to trusting earth women. Their primal reaction is to never be fooled by the cat people again.

It's time to disconnect from that correlation. As crazy as these taps seem, I am hoping that some will try doing them to see if it causes a shift in them. It may be a clue to balancing out female energy on earth. The cat people are not female and they are not cats. It is just a way that humans identify with them. If anyone dislikes cats, or gets extremely jealous or is attracted to exotic women, these taps may create freedom.

(Say each statement out loud three times while tapping on your head and say it a fourth time while tapping on your chest.)

"I release being enslaved by the cat people planet; in all moments."

"I release earth being enslaved to the cat people planet; in all moments."

"I release being manipulated by the cat people: in all moments."

"I release earth being manipulated by the cat people

planet; in all moments."

"I release the trauma of being taken to the cat people planet; in all moments."

"I release the anguish of being sold into slavery; in all moments."

"I recant all vows and agreements between myself and the cat people planet; in all moments."

"I recant all vows and agreements between earth and the cat people planet; in all moments."

"I remove all curses between myself and the cat people planet; in all moments."

"I remove all curses between earth and the cat people planet; in all moments."

"I dissolve all karmic ties between myself and the cat people planet; in all moments."

"I dissolve all karmic ties between earth and the cat people planet; in all moments."

"I remove all the shackles that the cat people planet has put on me; in all moments."

"I remove all the shackles that the cat people planet has put on earth; in all moments."

"I remove all the pain, trauma, burden and limitations that the cat people planet has put on me; in all moments."

"I remove all the pain, trauma, burden and limitations that the cat people planet has put on earth; in all moments."

"I withdraw all my energy from the cat people planet; in all moments."

"I withdraw all earth's energy from the cat people planet; in all moments."

"I take back all the joy, love, abundance, freedom, health, success, security, companionship, peace, life, wholeness, beauty, enthusiasm, contentment and confidence that the cat people planet has taken from me; in all moments."

"I take back all the joy, love, abundance, freedom, health, success, security, companionship, peace, life, wholeness, beauty, enthusiasm, contentment and confidence that the cat people planet has taken from earth; in all moments."

"I strip all the illusion off the cat people planet; in all moments."

"I release resonating with the cat people planet; in all moments."

"I release earth resonating with the cat people planet; in all moments."

"I release emanating with the cat people planet; in all moments."

"I release earth emanating with the cat people planet; in all moments."

"I remove all of the cat people planet from my sound frequency; in all moments."

"I remove all of the cat people planet from earths sound frequency; in all moments."

"I remove all of the cat people planet from my light body; in all moments."

"I remove all of the cat people planet from earth's light body; in all moments."

"I transcend the cat people planet; in all moments."

"Earth transcends the cat people planet; in all moments."

"I shift my paradigm from the cat people planet to joy, love, abundance, freedom, health, success, security, companionship, peace, life, wholeness, beauty, enthusiasm, contentment and confidence; in all moments."

"I shift earth's paradigm from the cat people planet to joy, love, abundance, freedom, health, success, security, companionship, peace, life, wholeness, beauty, enthusiasm, contentment and confidence; in all moments."

"I am centered and empowered in divine love; in all moments."

"Earth is centered and empowered in divine love; in all moments."

I am curious if you feel anything from doing these taps.

Evolving Beyond Selfless

Are you one of those people who gives until it hurts? You know. You are there for everyone in their time of need. You go the extra mile. You surprise others with little gifts. But on the rare occasion that you ask for help, there is little reciprocation. You are happy to give, and you are not trying to be a martyr, but you don't understand why it is so one-sided.

You may have set it up that way. Something in your energy may feel safe, more in control, or better about yourself if you are the one doing all the giving. It is a noble trait to be selfless. But there is step beyond selfless. There is giving to yourself and making yourself feel as good and empowered as you do for others.

The thing is that individuals are moving beyond group dynamics. Individuals are innately withdrawing their energy from all groups. So when you finally have the empowerment to offer a great group to others, they are too busy pulling their energy back to feed any into your group.

It is coming to a time when everyone is being empowered as an individual. It may shift the dynamics of all of humanity. It may feel uncomfortable perhaps but the self-empowerment is worth it. Everyone will have to jump on the bandwagon and start loving themselves as they love everyone else.

APPENDIX

Additional Taps:

Command Worthiness

(Say each statement three times while tapping on your head and say it a fourth time while tapping on your chest.)

"I declare myself a surrogate for humanity in doing these taps; in all moments."

"I release the aversion to worthiness; in all moments."

"I release being invested in unworthiness; in all moments."

"I release the repulsion between worthiness and monetary value; in all moments."

"I release the aversion to allot a monetary value to my worth; in all moments."

"I release being enslaved to unworthiness; in all moments."

"I release leaving my worth in the intangible realms; in all moments."

"I release the fear of tainting my worth with physicality; in all moments."

"I release the fear that my worth will be stolen from me; in all moments."

"I release the trauma of losing my worth; in all moments."

"I send all energy matrices into the light that steal my worth; in all moments."

"I command all complex energy matrices that steal my worth to be escorted into the light by my guides; in all moments."

"I send all energy matrices that negate my worth into the light; in all moments."

"I command all complex energy matrices that negate my worth to be escorted into the light by my guides; in all moments."

"I send all energy matrices into the light that diminish my worth; in all moments."

"I command all complex energy matrices that diminish my worth to be escorted into the light by my guides; in all moments."

"I take back my worth; in all moments."

"I remove all vivaxes between myself and unworthiness; in all moments."

"I remove all tentacles between myself and unworthiness; in all moments."

"I remove the claws of unworthiness from my beingness; in all moments."

"I remove all programming and conditioning that unworthiness has put on me; in all moments."

"I remove all engrams of unworthiness from my beingness; in all moments."

"I untangle myself from unworthiness; in all moments."

"I release identifying with unworthiness; in all moments."

"I release associating with unworthiness; in all moments."

"I send all energy matrices of unworthiness into the light; in all moments."

"I command all complex energy matrices of unworthiness to be escorted into the light by my guides; in all moments."

"I strip all illusion off of unworthiness; in all moments."

"I remove all masks, walls, and armor of unworthiness from my beingness; in all moments."

"I strip all illusion of unworthiness from my beingness; in all moments."

"I withdraw all my energy from unworthiness; in all moments."

"I release using unworthiness to wield superiority; in all moments."

"I release donning unworthiness as competition; in all moments."

"I release using unworthiness to gain favor with God; in all moments."

"I release using unworthiness as leverage; in all moments."

"I release using unworthiness as a decoy; in all moments."

"I recant all vows and agreements between myself and unworthiness; in all moments."

"I remove all curses between myself and unworthiness; in all moments."

"I release deeming worthiness as unfathomable; in all moments."

"I remove all blessings between myself and unworthiness; in all moments."

"I remove all curses between myself and unworthiness; in all moments."

"I shatter all glass ceilings on the worthiness that I will allow; in all moments."

"I release waiting to deem myself worthy; in all moments."

"I remove all repulsion between my worthiness and matter, energy, space, and time; in all moments."

"I release being rendered unworthy in matter, energy, space, and time; in all moments."

"I render matter, energy, space and time ineffective in

affecting my worthiness; in all moments."

"I sever all strings, cords, and wires between myself and unworthiness; in all moments."

"I dissolve all karmic ties between myself and unworthiness; in all moments."

"I remove all the pain, burden, and limitations that unworthiness has put on me; in all moments."

"I remove all the pain, burden, and limitations that I have put on all others due to unworthiness; in all moments."

"I release deeming myself or others unworthy; in all moments."

"I remove all the fear, futility, and illusion of separateness that unworthiness has put on me; in all moments."

"I remove all the fear, futility, and illusion of separateness that I have put on all others due to unworthiness; in all moments."

"I take back all that unworthiness has taken from me; in all moments."

"I give back to all others all that I have taken from them due to unworthiness; in all moments."

"I release resonating with unworthiness; in all moments."

"I release emanating with unworthiness; in all moments."

"I extract all unworthiness from my sound frequency; in all moments."

"I extract all unworthiness from my light emanation; in all moments."

"I extract all unworthiness from my whole beingness; in all moments."

"I shift my paradigm from unworthiness to worthiness; in all moments."

"I transcend all unworthiness; in all moments."

"I infuse worthiness into my sound frequency; in all moments."

"I infuse worthiness into my light emanation; in all moments."

"I am centered and empowered in worthiness; in all moments."

"I resonate, emanate, and am interconnected with all life in worthiness; in all moments."

-Freedom Health Success-

Release the Attachment to the Shackles

The reason more people aren't free is because they are emotionally attached to their shackles. We are no different than an abused animal that is fearful of coming out of its cage. Yet we are not apt to understand the nature of what the cage is because we have forgotten the freedom beyond the cage. If we lived in another time, how peculiar would it be to think of people sitting around and staring at a box on the wall all day? To them that would seem like a shackle. They would be right.

Here is to releasing humanity from shackles of all kinds. We don't need to realize what they are to release from them. Perhaps it is better if we don't. Because shackles have held us imprisoned in many ways: physically, emotionally, habitually and mentally. Here is to leveling the playing field so that free will has a chance by removing all shackles.

(Say each statement three times out loud while tapping on your head and say it a fourth time while tapping on your chest.)

"I declare myself a surrogate for humanity in doing these taps; in all moments."

"I release being enslaved to any and all shackles; in all moments."

"I release being dependent on any and all shackles; in all moments."

“I remove the glass ceiling of any and all shackles from my beingness; in all moments.”

"I release using any and all shackles to diminish myself; in all moments.”

"I release the genetic propensity to subscribe to any and all shackles; in all moments.”

“I remove all propensity to accept or wear shackles from my DNA; in all moments.”

“I remove the muscle memory of accepting shackles; in all moments.”

"I release using shackles as an excuse not to transcend; in all moments.”

"I release using shackles as a security blanket; in all moments.”

“I release confusing shackles for love or nurturing; in all moments.”

"I release being at the mercy of any or all shackles; in all moments.”

"I release using any and all shackles to feel safe; in all moments.”

"I release using any shackles to define myself; in all moments.”

“I dry up all psychic streams that keep me connected to

any shackles; in all moments."

"I withdraw all my energy from any and all shackles; in all moments."

"I release being manipulated, coerced, duped, corrupted or enslaved by any and all shackles; in all moments."

"I remove all vivaxes between myself and any and all shackles; in all moments."

"I remove all tentacles between myself and any and all shackles; in all moments."

"I remove the grip of any and all shackles from my beingness; in all moments."

"I collapse and dissolve all portals to any source that dispenses shackles; in all moments."

"I release perpetuating the limitations of any and all shackles; in all moments."

"I strip all illusion off of any and all shackles; in all moments."

"I remove all masks, walls and armor from the perpetuation of any and all shackles in any form; in all moments."

"I remove all masks, walls and armor that any and all shackles have put on me; in all moments."

"I eliminate the first cause in regards to being held by any and all shackles; in all moments."

"I remove all programming and conditioning that any and all shackles have put on me; in all moments."

"I remove all engrams of any and all shackles; in all moments."

"I remove all muscle memory of wearing any and all shackles; in all moments."

"I send all energy matrices into the Light and Sound that use any and all shackles to limit humanity; in all moments."

"I command all complex energy matrices that use any and all shackles to limit humanity to be escorted into the Light and Sound; in all moments."

"I send all energy matrices into the Light and Sound that perpetuate the use of any and all shackles; in all moments."

"I command all complex energy matrices that perpetuate the use of any and all shackles to be escorted into the Light and Sound; in all moments."

"I nullify all contracts with any and all shackles; in all moments."

"I nullify all contracts with everyone and everything that perpetuates any and all shackles; in all moments."

"I recant all vows and agreements between myself and any

and all shackles; in all moments."

"I collapse and dissolve all the limitations of any and all shackles; in all moments."

"I remove all curses between myself and any and all shackles; in all moments."

"I remove all blessings between myself and any and all shackles; in all moments."

"I dissolve all karmic ties between myself and any and all shackles; in all moments."

"I cut all the cords and ties to any and all shackles; in all moments."

"I remove all the pain, burden, limitations, and control that any and all shackles have put on me; in all moments."

"I remove all the pain, burden, limitations, and control that I have put on all others due to any and all shackles; in all moments."

"I take back all the joy, love, abundance, freedom, health, success, security, companionship, creativity, peace, life, wholeness, beauty, enthusiasm, contentment, spirituality, enlightenment, confidence, intellect, the ability to discern and empowerment that any and all shackles have taken from me; in all moments."

"I give back to all others; all the joy, love, abundance, freedom, health, success, security, companionship, creativity, peace, life, wholeness, beauty enthusiasm, contentment, spirituality, enlightenment, confidence, intellect, the ability to discern and empowerment that I have taken from them due to any and all shackles; in all moments."

"I convert all the dependency on shackles into exponential freedom; in all moments."

"I release resonating with any and all shackles; in all moments."

"I release emanating with any and all shackles; in all moments."

"I extract all shackles from my sound frequency and the universal sound frequency; in all moments."

"I extract all shackles from my light emanation and the Universal light emanation; in all moments."

"I shift my paradigm and the Universal paradigm from any and all shackles to exponential freedom; in all moments."

-Joy Love Abundance-

Abolish Every Kind of Slavery

(Say each statement three times while tapping continuously on your head and say it a fourth time while tapping on your chest.)

"We declare ourselves surrogates for humanity in doing these taps; in all moments."

"We release being impervious to any kind of slavery; in all moments."

"We release being deceived into any kind of slavery; in all moments.'

"We release the genetic propensity to be enslaved; in all moments."

"We release being stuck in the primal mode of being enslaved; in all moments."

"We release being shackled to any kind of slavery; in all moments."

"We release allowing any kind of slavery to be our common denominator; in all moments."

"We release being subjugated by any kind of slavery; in all moments."

"We release being circumvented by any kind of slavery; in all moments."

"We release feeling indebted to any kind of slavery; in all

moments."

"We nullify all contracts between ourselves and every form of slavery; in all moments."

"We dissipate all loyalty to any kind of slavery; in all moments."

"We remove all vivaxes between ourselves and every kind of slavery; in all moments."

"We remove all tentacles between ourselves and every kind of slavery; in all moments."

"We remove the claws of slavery from humanity and our personal beingness; in all moments."

"We release being ruled by any kind of slavery; in all moments."

"We remove all programming and conditioning that any kind of slavery has put on us; in all moments."

"We remove all engrams of slavery from our beingness; in all moments."

"We send all energy matrices that enslave us into the Light and Sound; in all moments."

"We command all complex energy matrices that enslave us to be escorted into the Light and Sound by our guides; in all moments."

"We0 send all energy matrices into the Light and Sound

that exemplify any kind of slavery; in all moments."

"We command all complex energy matrices that exemplify any kind of slavery to be escorted into the Light and Sound by our guides; in all moments."

"We recant all vows and agreements between ourselves and every kind of slavery; in all moments."

"We strip all illusion off of every kind of slavery; in all moments."

"We remove all masks, walls, and armor from every kind of slavery; in all moments."

"We shatter all glass ceilings that any kind of slavery has put on us; in all moments."

"We eliminate the first cause in regards to every kind of slavery; in all moments."

"We remove all curses between ourselves and every kind of slavery; in all moments."

"We remove all blessings between ourselves and every kind of slavery; in all moments."

"We strip all entitlement off of every kind of slavery; in all moments."

"We remove all the pain, burden, and limitations that every kind of slavery has put on us; in all moments."

"We remove all the fear, futility and unworthiness that

every kind of slavery has put on us; in all moments."

"We remove all the apathy, indifference, and devastation that every kind of slavery has put on us; in all moments."

"We remove all the rejection, abandonment, and illusion of separateness that every kind of slavery has put on us; in all moments."

"We remove all that we have put on all others due to any kind of slavery; in all moments."

"We take back all the joy, love, abundance, freedom, health, success, security, companionship, creativity, peace, life, wholeness, beauty, enthusiasm, contentment, spirituality, enlightenment, confidence, family, intellect, the ability to discern and empowerment that every kind of slavery has taken from us; in all moments."

"We give back all that we have taken from all others due to any kind of slavery; in all moments."

"We collapse and dissolve every kind of slavery; in all moments."

"We release resonating or emanating with any kind of slavery; in all moments."

"We extract every kind of slavery from our sound frequency; in all moments."

"We extract every kind of slavery from our light emanation; in all moments."

"We extract every kind of slavery from all 32 layers of our auric field; in all moments."

"We extract every kind of slavery from our whole beingness; in all moments."

"We abolish every kind of slavery as a construct; in all moments."

"We shift our paradigm from any kind of slavery to Love and Acceptance; in all moments."

"We transcend every kind of slavery; in all moments."

"We are centered and empowered in Universal Love and Spiritual Freedom; in all moments."

"We resonate, emanate, and are interconnected with all life in Universal Love, and Spiritual Freedom; in all moments."

-Freedom Health Success-

TESTIMONIALS

If you want to feel self-love and feel the abundance of all, to lose tons (I am not talking about body weight; I am talking about inner weight the kind that weighs us all down), I am so thankful to Jen for the help.

-Joy Love Abundance-

My life has themes and patterns. Well, I had gotten myself into a pattern that was no longer useful to me. That is where Jen comes in. She has a natural gift of "unsticking" us from our patterns and ourselves. To do that, she has to get creative and use methods that might seem unconventional, but they work. My session with Jen is unique to me, but what I can tell you is that she listens to her inner voice and does what she needs to do, so you can start to manifest the light that is within for all to see. Blessings to Jen for her bravery and fortitude when helping others.

-Freedom Health Success-

I don't know if this counts as a testimonial, and I don't send it to you out of any desire to be in your book, only to give you information that this exchange has really affected my life for the best. My story is similar to yours and I have been struggling for decades. Even though I have paid thousands of dollars for therapy and I'm a born-again Christian who has laid all the pain, and my personal part at the cross, still I could not find healing, and so I kept lamenting to our father for help. The Lord brought me to you, and you said once that as a Christian woman I could do your taps as prayers. I have done many of your Taps as prayers. I have woken up in the middle of the night in sweat-drenching nightmares reached out for you, did your Taps, and in the last six months since I found you, veils have been lifted left and right, and every day I get stronger. I am without a job; I've never had the money to pay you but I have asked the source who I see as the Lord bring to you what I could not. You have changed my life in ways I couldn't begin to list.

-Joy Love Abundance-

My healing session with Jen has reached into the deepest layers of causal suffering in my system, helping me profoundly. My mind and body are experiencing huge magnificent changes. Life force and wellbeing and clarity and love levels very increased!

-Freedom Health Success-

After many years of intense healing work and with some very challenging conditions that have never been resolved until now, I can say that her healing sessions are unique powerful pure and they WORK. I am eagerly inviting all my friends and family who desire true healing to experience her offerings.

-Joy Love Abundance-

Jen Ward's healing energy work is changing my life profoundly, and bringing her to your attention is a great pleasure and honor. I was one who thought that "answers" to my personal quandaries were received by diligent searching and disciplined spiritual attention. My work to believe in and discover. Well then there are nudges to follow, and I followed Jen's blog and thought a personal session with her might be a good thing. To express my gratitude and convey the miraculous benefits is a great challenge because real healing involves more than meets the eye, and there's no "therapy" I've encountered that means as much as our "releasing energy" sessions. To feature Jen and her loving work would be a blessing to mankind, sincerely. Thank you for this venue to express my gratitude to Jen!

-Freedom Health Success-

Rarely in life does one meet a person like Jen Ward. The impact she has had on countless lives is remarkable and immeasurable and cannot be denied. I cannot say that I know a more passionate person than Jen, and her message is one of healing and love. She has a unique perspective and is very enlightening.

-Joy Love Abundance-

I have been a student of ESP, the occult, and parapsychology since my first ESP experience at the age of ten. I am a spiritual writer and reader. I must tell you that I have NEVER met a more spiritual person than Jen Ward. If you are truly interested in exposing people to real spirituality, love, and knowledge of themselves and their relationship to God, there is no one I could recommend more highly than Jen Ward.

-Freedom Health Success-

Jen Ward is amazing. She handles everything with grace, loving kindness, and gentleness. Her wisdom and insight are some things that can be experienced by reading her work. She is inspirational. She is also loving, kind, graceful and so giving to others.

-Freedom Health Success-

Jen Ward has helped make me a better mother, wife, friend, and human being. She is the real deal. She has also helped my children and husband. Just when you think something can't be solved, Jen will be there to breakthrough whatever it is that prevents your evolution. She is AMAZING! Try a session and you will understand. The world is a better place because of Jen Ward.

-Joy Love Abundance-

A dear friend of mine referred me to Jen Ward. We have had two sessions thus far, and each time I felt what I believe to be stagnant energy exit directly through my chest and limbs. Her gifts go beyond spiritual healing; she cleanses your karma. She is powerful in a way that I never knew existed and, incredibly, with no pomp or ego.

-Freedom Health Success-

I attribute much of my success to coaches. These have included sports, career, sales, executive, and even resume coaches. However, the most powerful coach I have ever had has been Jen Ward of jenward.com. I have called her my energy coach for over three years. I'm not sure how she does it, but she can make me feel like a million bucks.

-Joy Love Abundance-

I believe in Jen Ward and her extremely high level of consciousness. Her love is bigger than global. Her story is one worth knowing. Jen gives to humanity a gift that is beyond compare.

-Freedom Health Success-

I went to Jen for neck trouble. I was scared because the pain was so intense at night I had trouble sleeping. I felt like my head wasn't sitting properly on my spine. I had spent years in and out of chiropractors' offices, but I wasn't in a position where I lived to see one, nor did I feel on an intuitive level that they could solve the problem at this point in my life. So I had a session with Jen, and it has been almost a week now, and I am free of the severe neck and back pain with only a memory of soreness. I'm grateful for Jen's work and these simple but profound taps.

Last night, in my evening contemplation, I had a possible solution to a situation I was working on in my own life, and I thought that I could message this possible fix to Jen Ward and see what she thought about it. But by then it was late, and I was tired so I didn't send the Facebook message. I just thought about it instead.

Well, all throughout the night, I came to realize that I was receiving inner instructions from none other than Jen Ward, and when I woke up, I woke up refreshed, and with a great solution for my situation! I also woke up an hour earlier than usual, full of energy, enthusiasm, and new hope!

This is amazing! Who do you know who can also do this? Isn't this usually reserved for the leaders who truly help restore the freedom of Soul? I believe it is.

Thank you, Jen!

I followed my spirit, which handed me a gift. My discussion with Jen evolved into some healing and clearing opportunities. In the middle of this, she suddenly said she was getting some sound waves and asked if I had sung as a kid, "We are marching to Pretoria," and I don't know why, but YES, we sang that as kids!!! I hadn't thought of that song in forever! And so I did taps on being a soldier. They were so helpful.

Working through stuff takes bravery for me. I am grateful for renewed self-trust and for Jen's in-the-moment immediacy of how she works. Thank you.

-Joy Love Abundance-

Jen is a friend, as well as a faithful healer, conduit, prolific writer, energy-sensor. I have worked with many folks in the healing profession—personally as well as professionally—and I have never encountered anyone who works with such immediacy of understanding and truth. It is fascinating to watch her work. Her deep understanding of the energetic nature of the universe lends itself to profound written and verbal exclamations. Plus, Jen has a wonderfully witty and wry sense of humor. Get to know her! Jen uplifts and helps a lot of people.

-Freedom Health Success-

Just had a really powerful healing session with Jen Ward. It reminded me who I am in the deepest way possible. Lifetimes and lifetimes were just illuminated and healed with the remembrance of that joyous, loving, light self, who can carry that into this world, not the other way around. That is my call to action and my call to just be. To emanate light and love for the entire universe. If you are feeling out of touch, in need of healing, or needing to release old ways of being, I highly recommend her.

-Joy Love Abundance-

I am an energy healer myself and have had many sessions with different healers. Today was one of the most powerful sessions I have ever experienced. Jen was able to take me deeper than others. Her ability to identify with me at such deep levels has already made such an intense difference. I just know that to be true. She is an amazing gift, and I truly honor her for the gift of healing she has achieved through her own work! If you are willing to go DEEP, please don't hesitate to connect with this Master Healer.

-Freedom Health Success-

Jen has just given me some priceless help, got me to tap for some health issues that would appear to have roots in previous lives. Starting to feel better already, my vision has become clearer and everything is brighter; can't wait to see what more wonderful effects I will get. Bless you Jen xxx

-Joy Love Abundance-

And my journey continues with each session I have with Jen Ward. As well, the results keep growing just as the effects and realizations of meditation stay with you after you have meditated. One continues to awaken, open, more and more as with each passing moment. Every session is powerful with Jen, and each session feels more powerful than the previous and today it felt like once again another layer was peeled away. Actually many. Once again, I felt a HUGE breakthrough. My heart is opening, and as a result, so is my hand. I feel I can hold hands with abundance, hold hands with love, I feel free! Thank you Jen...love you so.

-Freedom Health Success-

As a spiritual truth seeker, the thing I know is that many of our problematic issues are connected to previous lives where the curtain has been drawn and we can't see the direct cause of fears and anxieties. This is not kooky hearsay but documented reality, if one really wants to know their personal truth of troubling matters. I've experienced the benefits of numerous therapy sessions, but there comes a time when you know to follow your gut and be open to other possibilities. In heeding my inner guidance, I found jenward.com. Profoundly helpful--to the extent that I can risk any and all judgments--if just one individual is sparked and guided to consider Jen Ward's assistance. Suffering and living in the shadows of our best good can be dramatically eased and eliminated with understanding the puzzle pieces that created our present challenges, whatever they may be.

-Joy Love Abundance-

Remember John of God? I just had a session with Jen Ward and I got more out of one session with her than of all the times that I visited JOG in person. I've been to Brazil and Omega many times to see him and gave up. I would suggest you investigate her and consider sharing her gift with the rest of the world.

-Freedom Health Success-

First session with Jen this morning and I had no idea what to expect or how deep-seated the negative energy was held in my body until she began clearing the layers. Jen was able to get to the heart of the matter within the first 10-15 minutes! I've been through months of therapy that didn't come close to removing the blockages that Jen did in one hour, and she started the session knowing nothing about me! Amazing. Life-changing. Freeing. Jenuine. Above All, Love. Thank you, Jen!

-Joy Love Abundance-

I recently came across a woman, Jen Ward, who has a remarkable gift for healing. Because of her, I am finally able to "re-frame" a lot of issues in my mind that were totally crippling my life. To say I was skeptical when my fiancee told me about her would be an understatement. I'm fairly open-minded, but it took me six months before I finally booked an appointment with a "sound healer"—but I was blown away at how much we were able to work through in less than two hours!

I've been to traditional counselors, Christian counselors, military counselors, psychics, energy healers, hypnotists, counselors of various other religions—you name it—I've tried it. They all helped to various degrees, but I was amazed at the progress and emotional release I experienced with one session with this lady. I have found someone to help me overcome the obstacles that I've constructed for myself over the years, and I am looking forward to finally living the life that was intended for me. I'm not sure I've ever been this excited about living!

(Jen, if you see this, your method still seems a bit crazy to me, but it DEFINITELY works! Thank you!)

-Freedom Health Success-

Last week, my husband had a session with Jen on the phone. It wasn't two hours until he was telling me that he felt more "empowered" and had more energy. Today, he told me on my way home that he loved and missed me. When I did arrive home today he immediately wanted me to see that he had cleared off several large piles of papers from his desk. Those papers had been there in the same place for many years. That is a first I think. Thank you Jen Ward for all you do in the service of others.

-Joy Love Abundance-

I'd say the Jen Ward is the best thing to happen to me since I met my better half and got married. I HAVE NEVER promoted anyone's work, but this is life-changing for me.

With tears in my eyes I'm just now realizing the magnitude of what has happened to me. I will tell everyone for the rest of my life what MASSIVE HELP came through you, my humble friend.

-Freedom Health Success-

In my lifetime, I have not met another person on the level as Jen. She does her work by telephone, and I was surprised to notice she was really tuned in to know what was going on with me. I wish everyone who wants GROWTH would realize how worth it this is. I moved from thinking to being!

Well, I for one can certainly attest to the wonder of those private sessions! Those sessions are so valuable. I'm on a new road now after my session. So much so that I count that day as a starting point to a new me! My experience was also that you are a person who carefully safeguards the feelings of everyone you talk to and even just communicating with you opens the heart. I can't say enough about the LOVE you have in your heart, so pure and so giving, and I was the recipient! I think wonderful good thoughts about you and your mission.

-Joy Love Abundance-

Jen, the day of my session with you was like getting a new set of tires for my car. I still have to drive to my destination, but now I can get traction and no longer am prone to getting a flat as often. Thank you, dear Jen!

-Freedom Health Success-

I went back to work today, and my boss who is quite sensitive hugged on me lots! She said she could feel the LOVE coming fom me and good energy! So more confirmation that my energy shifted! I knew you were the person that would help me make a shift! Thank you!

I feel an inner peace that only comes from God the Good. Thanks for everything

-Joy Love Abundance-

Jen discovered the root cause of my almost tape-recorded type responses to living situations and helped me erase the tape and replace it with a vital response to a heart-felt concern someone was voicing. I don't know how she learned this stuff, for it comes natural to her, but it's perhaps because she's an empath. Anyone who is wondering, let me tell you, you will be so glad you discovered this key to a life of vibrancy, a life of loving God, and your fellow human beings and pets.

-Freedom Health Success-

I had the most wonderful realization today because of Jen, one of my emotional sores was "not being wanted" or "being left out." I thought over the years I had healed that tenderness, but a series of recent events bought it back up, and I realized there was more to be done. The exquisitely beautiful part of the event was the realization that the person who I felt was orchestrating the exclusion was really mirroring back to me an untruth I was holding in my consciousness. Jen, how beautiful is that! It felt like source love wanted me to see how I was wounding myself. I am so wrapped up in the wonder and love of it all that I could almost worship at the feet of the God Child who mirrored this back to me.

-Joy Love Abundance-

It matters not why I held or why others held me down so tightly at all. It matters not any of the whys, how-comes, or the who with any and all lifetimes! What has been released and transformed in Divine Love is the result and the only matter that matters! Wow! To be free is one thing, to know and feel it is another and an amazing gift to self! I am in a space of gratitude from this connection. I am bathing in awesome energy right now thanks to a wonderful, albeit at times very challenging, healing session with the very awesome Jen Ward. Her unique style is awesome, and I understood the reason for it. I must say Jen does remind me of only one other unique expression of all that is, and I so welcomed her straightforward approach. Jen is an amazing, gifted healer within divine love.

-Freedom Health Success-

I was wondering if you are part of my soul group because it struck me so profoundly when I heard your voice on the phone how familiar you sounded and felt. I have been going internal for a few days, meditating. I woke up at 4 a.m. the night before last and realized how light my body felt and teared up because I didn't even realize, even with doing energy work, how very heavy I had felt before. Thank you so much! That person is being so friendly to me now I don't know how to react. It feels so awkward. I feel so clear and centered in myself.

-Joy Love Abundance-

I feel balanced, grounded and patient in my own self. Things don't "eat" at me. I'm able to let them go. I'm understanding me better and feel like I have matured so beautifully. Frustrating things happen, but my approach is different. I'm above it. I reflect and can move on. I feel like I used to grab the pain and hurt and tuck it in my pocket before. It was clouding who I was and who I wanted to be. Thank you for everything! Our sessions are definitely not over.

-Freedom Health Success-

Releasing deeply engrained masochism: The operative word here for me is *deeply*. Yes, Jen Ward released deeply engrained masochism in me this morning! Wow! I am free! Words can never suffice or adequately articulate my gratitude for such a boon. Deeply rooted samskaras, thought processes, behavior patterns all wiped out in one fell swoop by a session with Jen. Lifetimes of pain and in this lifetime, the repeating of veiled notions, self-destructive behaviors all in which I gave away my power all too freely. With humility I give thanks, Jen.

-Joy Love Abundance-

I wanted to share with you and thank you for my freedom. I have been doing a lot of your taps that you share. I can't put into words how grateful I am. I have been afraid of the dark since I was a child because I have always felt a presence. It would physically disturb me in my sleep and I always felt watched. I was never sure what it was or care to know at this point, but I was never able to have a good night's sleep unless my husband or my dog shared the bed with me. So when I would go out of town, I would get terrible sleep, next to none. I would dread the idea of even falling asleep by myself.

It was also embarrassing for me to admit as an adult that I was terrified of the dark and of telling people why. I was afraid of sounding like a crazy person. Last week, I went out of town, and when it was time for me to go to bed, I wasn't afraid, and I slept the whole night without any disturbances. I never had a night's sleep like that away from home. It was amazing! I'm so grateful to have found you in my life. Thank you for sharing your gift; it is a rare and wonderful blessing!

-Freedom Health Success-

Why I like working with Jen: I was in Scientology for a while and had a tremendous amount of wins, gains and freedom from it, but for me, I noticed I was giving up my freedom to them as I was advancing. The reason I like working with Jen so much is that she intuitively knows much of their "tech," and I receive gains without giving up my freedom. Thank you, Jen! You're spot on!

-Joy Love Abundance-

Jen, I had a dream about you the other night. You did a session on the phone with me through my dream. You had a Belgian or Danish accent. Very interesting! You transmitted verbal recordings of what I went through with my miscarriage. It was healing and I thank you!

You are with me, healing in a transient way! You have the same strong love for all of humanity. And you give your whole heart to all of us, the same (strength) no matter who we are and how we react or how much we accept or don't accept that love.

-Freedom Health Success-

Jen, I have been noticing some interesting things since my session with you and coming here and doing the taps. I could swear these taps were for me. After I did them, I remembered that yesterday I didn't write because I burned both hands.

Then I read another post you had written before taking a nap and it felt like you had done psychic surgery on me in my sleep. I could hear your voice explaining something to me in detail with many examples flashing through my mind, and I was blown away. I woke up from the shame of what you were talking about and great remorse or embarrassment, and I fell back asleep again, and you continued to work on me. It was incredible.

-Joy Love Abundance-

Clear the Clouds of Self-Imposed Ceilings!

Unexpected, powerful, simply amazing! I was shocked at what Jen was telling me. I had no idea these things were actually holding me back! She gave me a new awareness and opportunity to embrace spiritual freedom like nothing else I have ever experienced. Thank you Jen, for your priceless gift of hope and your uniquely unselfish spirit of genuine healing.

-Freedom Health Success-

I want to start off by saying what an amazing person Jen is. She has so much love, yet she does not sugarcoat anything. That is what I love about her. She brings the truth, and it's like a much-needed slap in the face. It was for me! She brought to my attention that I go about getting things the wrong way (like a spoiled brat), which is true. This is something I'm glad she brought up because I couldn't see it before.

As soon as I saw that truth, I instantly wanted to be a better person. She also went on to tell me about my son and me; we weren't connecting as mother and son, but I never knew why this was. For her to know exactly what my situation is just amazes me. She just knows. She led me through some taps to help with this. They definitely helped. I feel so much closer to my son since the session. It's an awesome feeling, like a huge weight being lifted off. It's unexplainable.

Sharing this intentionally with all my friends and associates that are interested in releasing what no longer serves their highest good and offering an introduction to a most wonderful healer who can help you replace these worn-out concepts with ideas and belief systems that work. True. I introduce you now to Jen Ward. Friend her, visit her page. Many of her techniques are simply given, and she is available for private counseling as well. Give yourself a gift.

-Joy Love Abundance-

I experienced profound emotional release and clearing during a long-distance phone session with Jen Ward. Within 10 seconds her sounds cut through my pain body and expressed ancient grief. I wept, purified. She is firm, sharp, crystal clear. Her taps, healing. By the end, I was light, radiant, expansive. I highly suggest following her page, doing her taps and investing in a session if you are called. Be prepared for shift beyond expectation. Thanks for being, Jen.

-Freedom Health Success-

I have been following Jen's tapping posts for a while now and recently had a strong sense that I wanted to work with her to help me free up some limiting patterns around creative passion. I am thrilled to share that yesterday's session has already reaped benefits. The best way I can think to describe it is that I have a renewed sense of inner expansion, inner space within which to create. It's like clearing out a densely cluttered garage housing all sorts of unused and outdated items that had been impossible to even walk around in. Now I feel freed up, I can see where to put my worktable and materials, things of my choosing, rather than living with clutter someone else put there in another time. Perhaps it's coming present to the here and now rather than living in a shadowy past that was crowding out my life force. I anticipate that this is just the beginning of an inner flowering as the work and processes deepen.

Thank you, Jen, for sharing your healing insights and for being a playful channel for unconditional love.

-Joy Love Abundance-

Do you know the night after you posted the "Climbing in the Church Tower Dream," I had these PTSD nightmares that we're playing every night when I went to sleep. Previously, I had them under control for a couple of years. I desperately wanted this reoccurring nightmare record on the record player stopped! The living nightmare happened that night and I could not hide. Terrified within the dream, I grabbed a pair of cowboy boots and I went to the back of my cedar closet. I stepped into the cowboy boots and I wrapped myself in my best friend's fur coat. Then in the dream in my mind I screamed, Lord! Lord! Send me Jen! Alyssa. I didn't get to the last 'A' before I was awake. That was the last night of nightmares. I have slept eight or nine hours ever since. I don't know how to explain, but something in what you said told me that I could be awake in the nightmare, that I could face what was chasing me, or if I was really terrified and screaming in my dream, I could also stop screaming and ask for help. I woke the next morning and did the tap dancing prayers. Took a day for my head to stop feeling like a freight train wasn't running through it, but I'm so grateful for the peace that seems to have come over the entire energies of my household. Jen I send you love.

ABOUT THE AUTHOR

Jen Ward, LMT, is a Reiki Master, an intuitive and gifted healer, and an innovator of healing practices. She is a prolific writer and has written seven books to date with many more on the way. She is at the leading edge of energy work, providing a loving segue for her techniques to clients, enabling them to cross the bridge of self-discovery with her. Her passion is to empower individuals in their own healing journey, so they can remain in their center every step of the way.

While attending the Onondaga School of Therapeutic Massage, she was first introduced to energy work. It soon became second nature for her to help identify and remove energy blocks from clients. She is highly proficient at tuning into individuals' specific needs to release their issues, allowing their own body to make the energetic changes necessary to return to a greater sense of ease. Her ability to pick up many different modalities as second nature is another aspect of her profound gifts.

Jen is considered a sangoma, a traditional African shaman, who channels ancestors, emoting sounds and vocalizations in ceremonies. An interesting prerequisite to being a sangoma is to have survived the brink of death. When Jen was first approached with the knowledge of being a sangoma, she had not yet fulfilled this prerequisite. However, in April 2008, when she came back to society on the brink of starvation as a result of traumatic involuntary imprisonment, the qualification had been met. She returned to the world of humanity a devout soul inspired to serve.

Her special abilities have also allowed her to innovate a revolutionary technique for finding lost pets by performing an emotional release on the animal. Using this method, she has successfully reunited many lost pets with their owners.

Jen currently works as a long-distance emotional release facilitator, public speaker, and consultant. Her special modality encompasses a holistic overview of her clients from all vantage points, including their physical, emotional, causal, and mental areas, ultimately benefiting their work, home, family, and especially spiritual lives.

You can find Jen at www.jenward.com

OTHER BOOKS BY JEN WARD

Enlightenment Unveiled*: Expound into Empowerment.* This book contains case studies to help you peel away the layers to your own empowerment using the tapping technique.

Grow Where You Are Planted: *Quotes for an Enlightened "Jeneration."* Inspirational quotes that are seeds to shift your consciousness into greater awareness.

Perpetual Calendar*: Daily Exercises to Maintain Balance and Harmony in Your Health, Relationships and the Entire World.* 369 days of powerful taps to use as a daily grounding practice for those who find meditation difficult.

Children of the Universe. Passionate prose to lead the reader lovingly into expanded consciousness.

Letters of Accord*: Assigning Words to Unspoken Truth.* Truths that the ancient ones want you to know to redirect your life and humanity back into empowerment.

The Do What You Love Diet: *Finally, Finally, Finally Feel Good in Your Own Skin.* Revolutionary approach to regaining fitness by tackling primal imbalances in relationship to food.

Affinity for All Life: ***Valuing Your Relationship with all Species.*** This book is a means to strengthen and affirm your relationship with the animal kingdom.

The Wisdom of the Trees. If one is struggling for purpose, they can find love, and truth by tuning into the *Wisdom of the Trees.*

Chronicles of Truth. Truth has been buried away for way too long. Here is a means to discover the truth that lies dormant within yourself.

Healing Your Relationships. This book is a means to open up communications and responsiveness to others so that clarity and respect can flourish again in society.

How to Awaken Your Inner Dragon: ***Visualizations to Empower Yourself and the World.***

Collecting Everyday Miracles: ***Commit to Being Empowered.*** This book is a thought provoking means to recreate the moment of conception with everyday miracles. It is through gratitude and awareness. This is what this book fosters.

All of Jen's books are available at http://www.jenward.com/jens-books/

CPSIA information can be obtained
at www.ICGtesting.com
Printed in the USA
LVHW08s1156141018
593564LV00034B/1292/P

9 781542 359030